SECRETS OF THE SIX FIGURE YOGA TEACHER

How to Make Real Money by Leading the Journey to Health and Enlightened Living

CATE STILLMAN

A free gift from Cate to break your glass ceiling:

6-Figure Yoga Teacher TOOLKIT

- ***Video Training***
- ***6-Figure WORKBOOK***
- ***1-1 Career Assessment & Consultation***

Find it here:

http://www.yogahealthcoaching.com/toolkit

If your actions inspire others to dream more, learn more, do more, and become more, you are a leader.

John Quincy Adams

A leader is best when people barely know he exists, when his work is done, his aim fulfilled, they will all say: we did it ourselves.

Lao Tzu

Contents

Dedicated to the those who are willing to lead the way, guiding people to thrive in their bodies and their lives.

1: The Career Secret of Successful Yoga Teachers

Commitment + Leadership = Success

Jen was a great yoga teacher. She got into yoga–not to become a teacher–but because the practice of yoga had changed her life. When Jen went to her first class, she had no idea that yoga would become the central pillar of her life. She tried a few teachers until she found her first true teacher, Joanne. Joanne seemed to know exactly what she was feeling ... and how to feel better. Her yoga teacher had an understanding of how bodies work and also how to practice yoga, to experience positive emotions as the baseline experience. For the first time in her life, Jen felt good in her body, happy in her life, and knew the wisdom of yoga would keep unfolding over the years of her life ahead. She wanted to live a wise life, a good life.

After years of enjoying being a student, Jen became a teacher. As a teacher, Jen grew a following. When Covid-19 shut down her studio and yoga classes went online a few of her students stuck with her connecting through Zoom. The connection made a difference. Others drifted away. Jen noticed that her yoga practice was the best pillar of her life in the unpredictable future.

She also noticed her friends ate more, drank more and smoked more from the stress. Jen was more appreciative of the prior investments she made in yoga... the time, the intention, the money she'd invested were paying off more in her life, with each passing year. She felt better than ever. The pandemic was an exhale, a slowing down, a turning inward.

Jen started to wonder ... why do some people, like myself, invest so heavily in wellness wisdom? Why are some of my students committed to their body goals, and others seem to dabble with wellness wisdom? How do I help people with all that I know? How do I accelerate people's path to commitment? Can I encourage people to better understand their choices today affect their tomorrow? How to I guide people to experience what I'm experiencing... the amazingness of feeling good - without them needing to become yoga teachers? Jen reflected that body wisdom is truly the best life investment and commitment she had made. She wouldn't trade it for the world. How could she help those that were currently suffering with mental, emotional and physical health issues?

Then, Jen met me.

This book is our conversation.

How to Lead Your Yoga Career to Financial Success

Each week I talk to very skilled yoga teacher professionals. I've been touched by their care, their wisdom, their drive and their skill. Yet, something is missing.

What is missing?

Often, holistic wellness professionals don't know how they can offer the most transformational value to their students. There are gaps. Gaps in their student's commitment. Gaps in using technology and using physical space. Gaps in developing an experience to guide people into their potential. Gaps in turning healing skills into a package to lead to results and truly be a transformative guide.

Gaps are gold mines of opportunity.

In this book, I'll show you how to mine for the gaps where you are leaving both client results and money on the table. When you close those gaps, you'll be doing the best work of your life, have the flexibility you want in your lifestyle, and be growing towards financial freedom. You'll get my best, current insights.

I'm known for being a very financially successful yoga teacher and wellness community developer–both locally and online. I'm also known for telling you exactly how it is. I'm a futurist in the field of guiding transformation with yoga and Ayurveda, with over 20 years at the helm of Yogahealer. I love to be invaluable to yoga teachers and holistic wellness pros, as I've been both.

If you aren't living your dream, you are less of an asset to your client community. You need to thrive–personally, professionally, and financially. If that is your goal, read on.

What is Your A to B?

Where is your value now?

If wellness isn't just a hobby for you, we need to talk money.

Professionals exchange value for value. The more value you can exchange, arguably, the more success you experience in your career.

With the fast pivot to online classes during the pandemic, many yoga teachers got confused about their value. More than ever they were competing for their students' attention with just about every other yoga teacher on the planet. Not to mention Youtube ... and other major free platforms providing free classes.

Where is your value now?

I'll cut to the chase. Your biggest value lever is to lead the journey. The journey to what? The journey from where your students or clients are now through an entire evolution, an entire transformation. An A to B. Meaning, now they are at A. A is usually struggling with the symptoms from underlying chronic, systemic inflammation. This may appear as stress in the mind, being over-scheduled, depression, overwhelm, carrying weight, immune issues, trouble sleeping, trouble digesting–aka bloating, the list goes on. The habits of A often involve late nights, snacking, always being busy, disruptions from screen time, caffeine for energy, and for a few, alcohol or weed to wind down.

How do you guide them to feeling great?

What is B? B is feeling great. Physically strong. Well rested. Deeply nourished. Dynamically engaged with their goals, their friends, their body and their whole life. B is having habits, automated habits, that reduce chronic systemic inflammation. At B, your clients are sleeping well, eating clean, digesting with ease. They are resilient and adaptable, and experience a baseline of positive emotions throughout the day, everyday.

That is a transformation. That is a solid A to B.

And if you are a yoga teacher or wellness pro worth your salt, chances are you can lead that journey right now. Maybe with a small potent dose of specialized training - in how to lead a journey to results - you could fill in some gaps to be incredibly effective.

Most wellness pros operate on a transactional business model. Their students pay by the class or series. Wellness pros often charge by the consult. This isn't a package that leads to results. Wellness pros are taught how to evaluate with a client what are their health issues, what are their health goals, and how to package based on results.

The local and global marketplace can make or break your dreams. If you shift from a transactional to a transformational business model - you uplevel yourself out of general competition. You simplify your marketing needs. You work with a set number of clients to hit your income target.

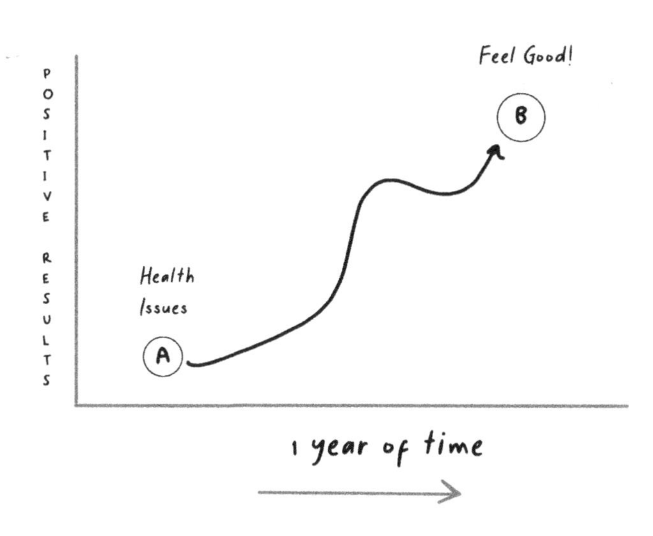

How Public Yoga Classes fit into Yoga Teacher's Financial Success

In the hundreds of yoga teachers I've talked to about their income streams this is a typical snapshot:

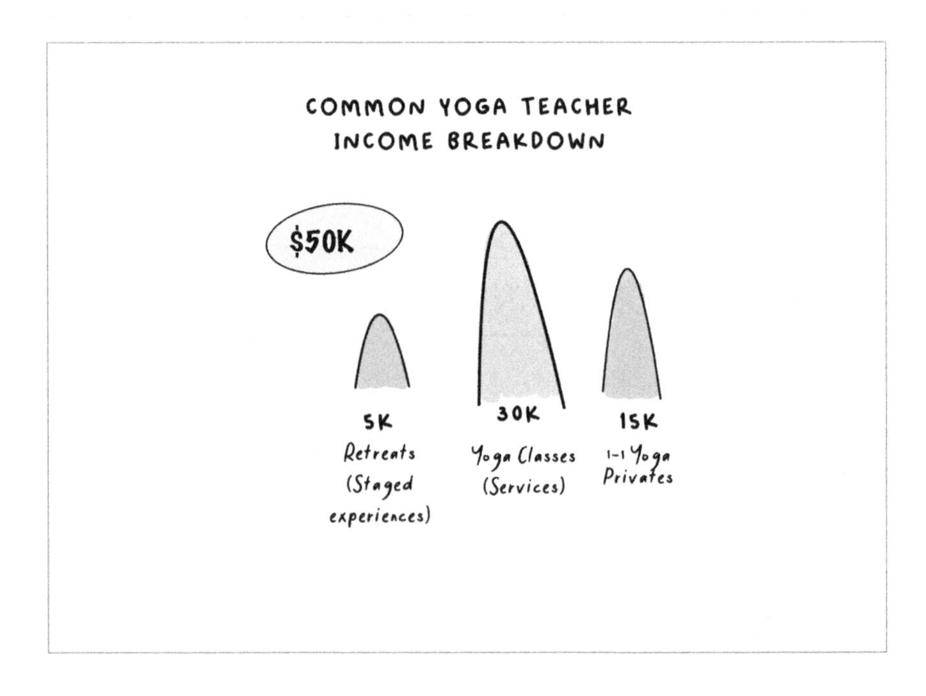

There are a few problems with this transactional business model. The first problem is no results-based package. No transformational journey. No invested commitment from the students. The second problem is there is no scalability for easily growth. The third problem is there is no service that leverages the teacher to leverage their lifestyle wisdom. Let's solve these problems.

As a package a transformative journey is an opportunity to lead. As an added income stream, the package is an upsell.

An upsell?

An upsell is when a client purchases something of a higher value and higher cost for an even better product or service. But let's start with the role of yoga classes, and then talk about your upsell.

Your public yoga classes serve the purpose of nurturing students through the phase of growing to like yoga, to know yoga and to trust yoga. In the process, your public classes give your students the possibility of getting to know, like and trust you. To resonate with you. To gain directly from your body wisdom.

To package a journey means to build an experience that is truly transformative. Transformation takes time. I recommend building a package with a year long journey.

If you can lead a journey, a transformational journey, you can make a great living and experience a lucrative lifestyle. I grew Yogahealer 50% during the pandemic, because I had an upsell that met the needs of people wanting to become resilient and thrive in an upbeat online community through the pandemic. I had set myself up to lead transformational journeys and people were ready to invest.

The upsell to the transformative journey can never go out of style. It'll never be too late to lead a journey with committed members to truly transformational results.

Why not?

Because the impulse to evolve is part of human nature. And those that can guide us to evolve are worth investing time with.

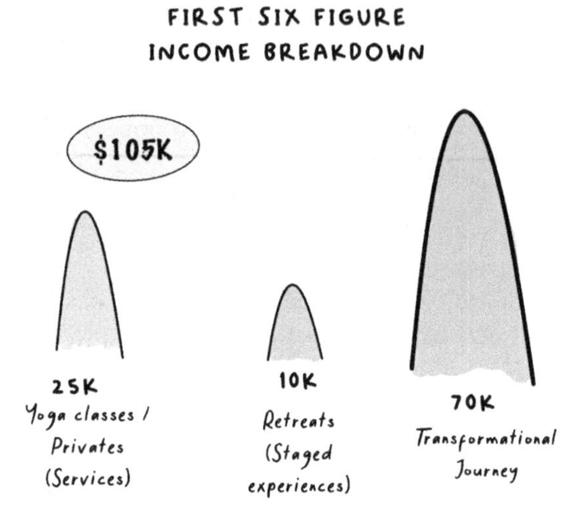

The enrollment on the journey permits you to work to results straightaway. Momentum builds. Leading invites you to create the infrastructure for your group to thrive.

Before we figure out the who and the what ... let's start with you.

- Your journey is the key.
- Your journey is the what.
- You need skills in packaging your journey.

Then, you'll need skills in attracting, engaging and enrolling your members. These skills aren't optional anymore. Many yoga studios learned early on that Yoga Teacher Trainings were a breadwinner that kept the studio in business. In the early days, studios could also depend on retail as a breadwinner, but as that went online, that income stream dried.

So, you need new skills.

That's normal. Growth generally requires your growth. You have to reprioritize your time for these new skills. These skills are leverageable–meaning the better you get at them, the more time you'll have for your life. And you need time for your life. Your thriving lifestyle is what attracts people to you. You are the product.

Your Business is Your Leadership Development Program

As a leader, you are the living results of the transformation. You are the product. Therefore, you must treat yourself as the product. You should be well rested. You should be deeply nourished. You should have the time of your life and live your purpose. Your self care should become exquisite yet uniquely your style. You will model the way. You become the leader of the way.

This has nothing to do with chasing perfection or perfectionism.

This has everything to do with you being you and your personal integrity. The more integrity you have, the easier it is for people to engage with your resonance. This isn't about purity or abstinence. You leading the way is leading the best way you can, with what is truly working for you in real time. You'll be guiding your people to experience your level of thrive with more speed and ease by addressing the key factors that work.

As a leader already, you are doing this. With the right business model and follow through on enrollment, you'll have freedom to be your best you. The two aspects–being the product and leading the journey–

become one in the same. Both aspects continually hold you to a higher standard for yourself. And that is yoga.

I speak from many years of experience. I tried purity and chastity and abstinence. I tried rebelling too. When you lead with authenticity, vulnerability and living wisdom ... you will gain traction.

If you let yourself get caught up in the busyness, or wired and tired, or fat and inflamed, you make your success too hard. You can't sacrifice your quality of life. Or your practice, your health. Or your time with your kids or parents. Or travel. Or meditation. Or whatever really lights you up.

To truly guide a transformational journey that earns a pretty penny–you need to be all in. You need to live up to your potential. No B.S ... no halfway. You're the guide. The leader. There is no way around it. To me, that is the beauty of the attention economy. You need to be worth paying attention to. When that happens, people invest. You live the results. That generates magnetism with people who are looking for that - whether they are aware of it or not. You represent.

> Representing the results is a serious deal. You'll clear up a handful of personal integrity issues. Don't take it personally. Purification through leadership happens.

Many yoga teachers are bumping their heads on a financial glass ceiling. Many are in a negative feedback loop of trading time–their most sacred possession–for not enough money to give them the lifestyle they truly want to live.

Over time, the loop spins into stress, from being out of integrity with the habits they know fuel their bodies and souls. At worst, they can end up with the same chronic stress issues as the clients they most want to guide. This is due to the wrong business model.

So what's the simplest key to success?

A key unlocks a door.

First check out what the key that unlocks your next level of success is not.

1. You don't need to sell online classes.
2. You don't need to become more popular or post on social media a few times a day, or run ads.
3. You don't need a pricey website.

The big key is the business model.

If you know the have the right business model, where you lead the journey to results, what is possible is a successful career on all fronts, including a lucrative lifestyle.

What is also possible for you is more time. Living in integrity with your wisdom. Only working with committed members. Less busyness. Less stress. More transformation. More impact. Earning more. Working less.

The business model is what leads the journey. I'll show you how. Before we get there–a quick review on what a business model is. Your business model is how you exchange services and products for money. If your business or career isn't set up to free up your time, you can't move your life forward. You can't be as good as you could be at what you do.

You can devote your full ability to getting results for your invested members. Why do I call them members, rather than students? Good question.

Members belong. Most students or clients come and go without commitment. Membership has an invested commitment. Commitment is necessary for transformation. Transformation is worth the commitment and has a strong return on the investment.

Thus, the business model is to lead the journey through a transformation. Most journeys, like most super solid yoga teacher training programs, take a year. My yoga teacher training was a solid two years at the Iyengar Yoga Institute from 1999-2001. Then I studied with John Friend for years before I earned certification in Anusara

Yoga. Transformation takes time, it takes practice, and is always faster within a transformational community.

> I'm not suggesting you build a BIG membership community. Unless you like big. Most yoga teachers and wellness pros I work with prefer a smaller group that is more committed, and more invested. Either way, there is leverage in terms of money and time.

The good news is now you know the key. Now I can show you, step by step, how to set yourself up for the best work of your life.

Financial Success

My name is Cate Stillman, I kicked off Yogahealer.com in 2001. This was eons ago in internet years. I devoted my life to personal and planetary thrive, beginning in high school. By my mid-20s I left a career in global environmental policy to work in wellness and enlightenment wisdom.

I quickly became more financially successful than my yoga teacher colleagues. As I earned more, I prioritized my lifestyle business. I wanted to live my best life now. And, I wanted good investments that enhanced my lifestyle. My personal version of that lifestyle dream includes living in two countries, two cultures, two climates, with two languages. My lifestyle has a lot of biking, skiing, river running, and surfing with my core people. For the last decade I've spent part of each year surfing in the subtropics.

With my earnings, I've purchased highly desirable real estate and maxed out my retirement tax benefits. I love being a mom and modeling the way for my girl. I love earning well so that I can afford lovely homes, make strong investments, fuel my family's dreams, and do the work that matters most without concern for money.

Even more importantly, I live a life of higher purpose, of dharma. I have a bigger, deeper more positive impact year over year with my members. I am more effective at what I do in growing people into leaders. I'm also well rested, fit, and deeply nourished. My personal health keeps improving. I'm at my fighting weight. I'm inspired. I'm focused. I'm productive. I'm effective in my work guiding people through transformation–both in health and career. These are signs of having a business model and lifestyle model that works for me.

> The right business model that works for your lifestyle makes your success. The wrong business model that doesn't work for your lifestyle will eventually break you.

Part of my personal purpose is to help yoga teachers and wellness professionals thrive. You need a business model that works for your lifestyle. Our communities rely on wellness pros to lead them to thrive. The degree to which *you* are thriving is the degree to which you can *lead*. Below is an example of a member becoming a leader:

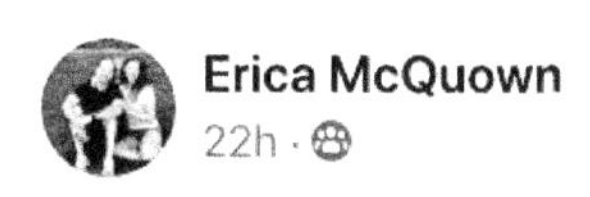

Feeling so incredibly grateful for this program and format.

My goal for the year was to double my revenue of last year. And I just hit it! Halfway through the year - 6 months into the program.

What's fantastic is that I will onboard my last group in August, and then the rest of the year is setting the stage for next year, when my goal is to double again. And I totally see the possibility of this happening. This also allows for maternity leave with my third baby due in October.

Beyond the discomfort I've shared when reaching my edge, this largely feels like it's allowing for easeful living with the appropriate amount of growth 😉 Allowing to balance all the aspects of motherhood, while creating a sustainable practice and serving my larger community.

Don't worry, I'll be back sharing my lows again when they come. For now riding the high of gratitude! 🙏💖

Carolyn Lang, Amy Heilman and 3 others 2 Comments Seen by 46

Leading by doing is most effective. I'll show you how to lead and to earn for leading the journey. You can unlock your potential to thrive as a yoga teacher. Your creative potential. Your wisdom. Your unique ability. Next, you need to get answers from within.

2: The Health Issues of Your Yoga Students

Health Issues Facing Modern Humans

Before we get into the right career model for yoga teachers ... let's first review what is happening with people today. The majority of people today are developing systemic inflammation year over year. The results of chronic systematic inflammation are devastating.

Unless you understand how inflammation develops in the mind and in the body–you aren't prepared to meet the needs of modern yoga students. Which means if you want to earn your keep, you should learn how yoga on and off the mat eats inflammation for breakfast.

Dr. Pahwa, who headed a 2020 NIH global Chronic Inflammation summarizes the problem below:

"Chronic inflammatory diseases are the most significant cause of death in the world. The World Health Organization (WHO) ranks chronic diseases as the greatest threat to human health. In recent estimates by Rand Corporation, in 2014 nearly 60% of Americans had at least one chronic condition, 42% had more than one and 12% of adults had 5 or more chronic conditions. Worldwide, 3 of 5 people die due to chronic

inflammatory diseases like stroke, chronic respiratory diseases, heart disorders, cancer, obesity, and diabetes."[1]

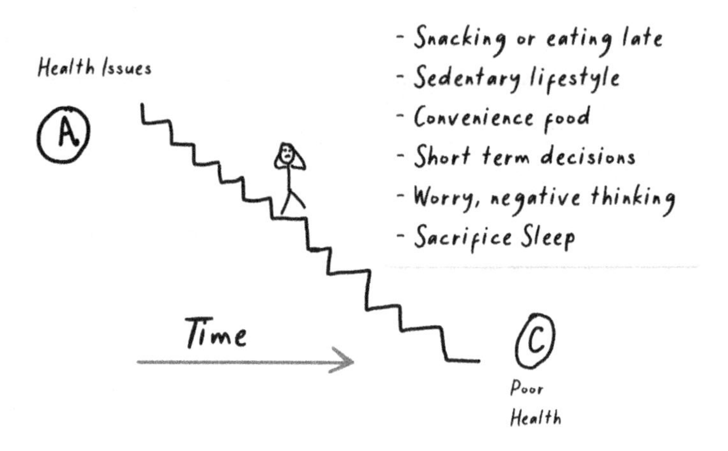

What? Three out of five people on the planet today will die of the diseases caused from chronic, systemic inflammation? And wait - cancer is due to chronic inflammation? And these diseases are preventable?

Chronic systemic inflammation is formed through inflammatory habits. Let's make sure you can recognize the symptoms and the habits in your students.

Chronic Inflammation and Needing to Lose Weight

In the US, the global trendsetter of modern disease, more than two-thirds (68.8%) of adults are considered overweight or obese. More than one-third (35.7%) of adults are considered obese. Almost 3 in 4 men (74%) are considered overweight or obese.

Being overweight is simply hard on the body and hard on mental and emotional health. The weight signifies the body has more matter than it can digest. For the body and mind, higher quantity of inputs means lower quality of outputs. When the output is your energy, your mood, and the shape you're in, the stakes for high quality, low quantity inputs in very high.

The excess mass within cells, and excess white fat cells, create a toxicity within the body. The body is a system. Inefficiency, due to poorly digested intercellular materials generates inflammation. When the habits of an excessive weight pattern continue over time, inflammation goes chronic. The body loses efficiency, intelligence and resilience.

Not all chronic inflammation shows up as excess weight. But, all of excess weight is a sign of chronic inflammation.

Did your great grandparents have chronic inflammation? How would you know? Were they overweight? When you look back at old photographs, one of the first thing most people notice is that almost no one was carrying extra weight. Those folks are lean, lithe, hardworking peeps. They ate two or three times a day. Snacks and supplements were *not* on the menu. Real food was the only option, and it wasn't usually wasted inside or outside of the body. Screens weren't around. Time was spent looking at the night sky, which was visible before light pollution.

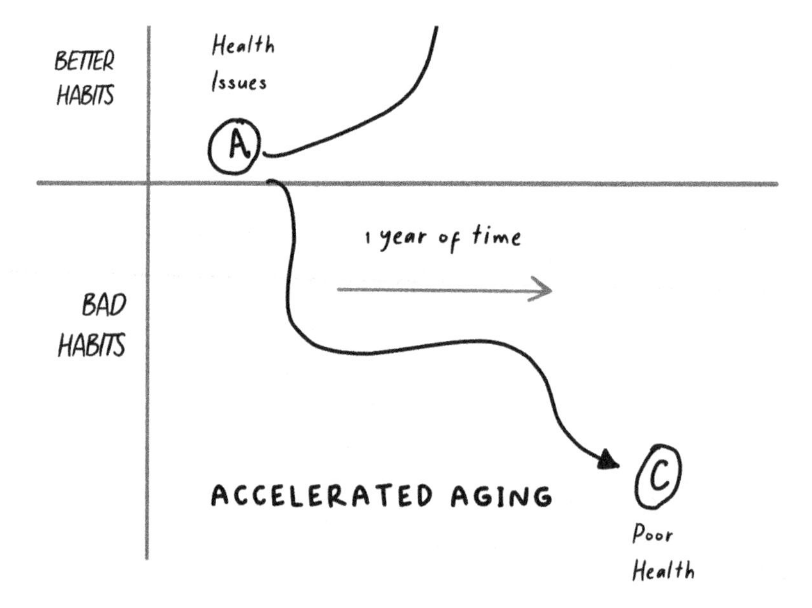

Times have changed.

Remember what people's bodies looked like before processed food, convenience food, late nights, habituated snacking, and loads of sedentary screen time. Knowing what your students are up against is important for guiding them to personal success and body wisdom.

Accepting what we're up against - from the modern food industry to the bombardment of drug-pushing commercials and advertisements - is one of the pivotal steps for you to be of true service to your yoga students.

Symptoms of Chronic Inflammation

How do you know if your students have chronic systemic inflammation? Below is a list of symptoms. Read them carefully while thinking of specific yoga students you are teaching.

Symptoms of Chronic, Systemic Inflammation:

- Fatigue
- Overwhelm
- Anxiety
- Depression
- Irritability
- Brain fog
- Difficulty sleeping
- Overall heaviness
- A coating on your tongue
- Stiff joints upon arising
- Difficulty making decisions
- Bloating
- Poor digestion

- Constipation
- Heartburn
- Snot
- Allergies
- Cravings for filler foods (poor nutrient density)
- PMS, fibrocystic breasts, and hard periods
- Cellulite, man boobs and spare tires
- Blood sugar spikes and crashes
- Emotional eating
- General Pain including headaches
- Susceptibility to illness, viruses and flus

You need to know these symptoms. As you can see, the symptoms range from digestion to emotions to endocrine system. Once inflammation has been long enough and chronic enough, the body develops disease–from cancer to heart disease to autoimmune disease. All of the major killers right now have their root in chronic systemic inflammation.

I find most people, even those who aren't overweight, have chronic inflammation due to impact of stress, information overload, not enough sleep, and a lack of a relaxing rhythm in their daily life.

Dr. Pahwa of the NIH global Chronic Inflammation study came to this conclusion: "*Furthermore ,the prevalence of diseases associated with chronic inflammation is anticipated to increase persistently for the next 30 years in the United States.*"[1]

Sounds like the problem is only getting worse. The problem with chronic inflammation is that it makes us less able to respond to the pattern of too much. What goes undigested builds up over time, and slowly destroys the natural intelligence inherent in our design.

Epidemic levels of chronic inflammation are a modern phenomenon. Chronic inflammation isn't new to the human species, but with processed food, a sedentary lifestyle, excess food availability, and eating more calories later in the day, we've become a bloated species that is challenged by premature degeneration.

When I embarked on my holistic body wisdom journey, I dove into yoga and it's sister science–Ayurveda. Ayurveda has a term that names the precursor to chronic inflammation. The term is "ama". It means "undigested". If a person develops a regular habit of putting too much into their body or mind, the body and mind can't keep up with digestion. The residue is toxic. That which you don't digest, puts a load on your system. With time, it feels like life is on top of you.

INFLAMMATION EQUATION

HOW CHRONIC INFLAMMATION
BECOMES CHRONIC DISEASE

As a yoga teacher and Ayurvedic practitioner I found that I could make a big dent in the chronic inflammation pattern by working with committed students, on the habits of yogis–the Body Thrive habits - over a year of time. A year is a cycle around the sun–a journey through the ups and downs of life, an escorted voyage through the seasons, the annual rhythm.

POTENTIAL TO THRIVE

Chronic inflammation is caused by daily habits that generate inflammation.

> The Buddha said life is suffering. He didn't say life is unnecessary suffering. The predictable habits that generate chronic inflammation cause unnecessary suffering. It's time to stop the madness.

What happens when chronic inflammation is worsened by the habit patterns that developed it in the first place? This pattern is accelerating aging. People don't know their habits are the core of their problems. Or if they do how to design a better experience from their habits. Chronic health issues turn into a chronic disease, due to the habits underlying the health issues. In a year - you can make a dent in people's health issues - in their chronic inflammation. In one year. That's not very long.

The opposite is also true.

In a year, people can gain more weight, more stress, more inflammation and go further into disease development. In the image below, notice how chronic symptoms over time become serious diseases. Serious diseases are difficult to cure. Some are incurable. However, almost all of the time their initial symptoms are relatively easy to reverse with the right leadership and guidance.

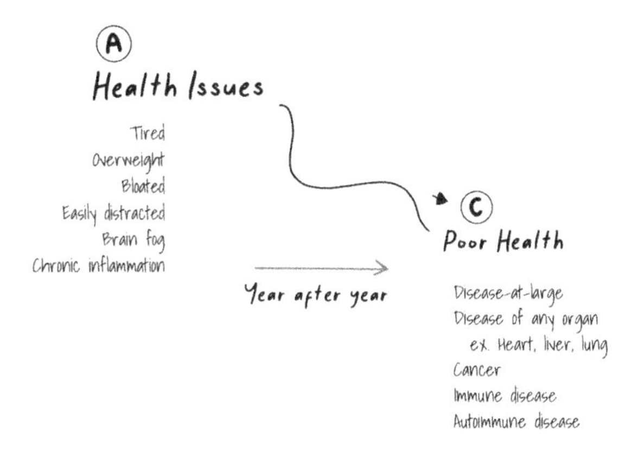

Most yoga teachers get into teaching to guide students into their potential. Their potential health, body confidence, resilience and adaptability. Understanding the habits that cause chronic inflammation isn't generally taught in yoga teacher training.

However, the habits of yogis must be taught to aspiring yoga teachers and students. We live in a culture that is increasingly settled into the habits that breed chronic inflammation. Most of your yoga students are looking for guidance to feel better. That guidance needs to be at the level of habit evolution.

Yogis have a codified daily routine, a living rhythm, that directly counteracts and uproots the pattern of chronic inflammation. It's part of the yogic wisdom tradition. We'll get to those habits later. Now, let's address the elephant in the room.

Yoga Habits are Anti-Inflammatory

Whatever imbalance your students have–whether it's their weight, their sleep, their immune system, their digestion - you will have a hard time guiding them to results faster, unless you guide them to smarter daily habits. The habits the yogis have always had.

> Healing is a matter of time, but it is sometimes also a matter of opportunity.
>
> Hippocrates

Think of the clients or students you have, that have a hard time going to bed early. Think of those who consistently eat a heavier or later dinner. Think of those who don't feel light, refreshed or rested when they wake up. Which of their daily habits are out of sync?

Out of sync habits disorganize the organism. We are creatures who evolved with a rhythm, the circadian rhythm. Those who go against the rhythm suffer eventually from chronic, systemic inflammation. Modern habits are out of sequence with circadian rhythm.

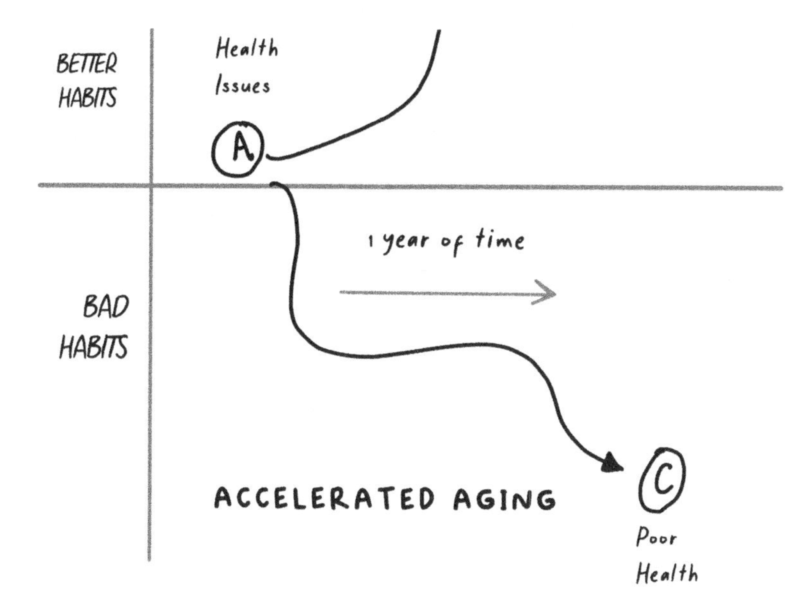

By the time they drop into yoga class hoping for relief, their core momentum is arhythmic. Unless you can help them with their core daily habits, the yoga will be a bandaid solution. You've probably witnessed this before. The student arrives stressed, bloated, wired and tired. They experience a prana-filled transformation during class. They go home and eat a heavy meal, perhaps overeat again, while enjoying a glass or two of wine. Rinse and repeat with time, and your yoga classes can't make much of a dent in the pattern.

The good news is ... the habits of yogis are right there for you to guide them to feeling good.

Habits are cultural. Modern people have habituated stress, busyness, negative emotions, sedentary lifestyle, and overeating. Bodies can't thrive with those habits. Our culture is out of sync, violating the fundamental rhythms of human health. Until the post-electricity modern era, humans lived in sync with circadian rhythm. The human body evolved over hundreds of thousands of years synchronized by the rhythm of the sun rising and setting. We are a diurnal, not nocturnal, species. In rhythm we thrive. Out of rhythm, we invite disease.

There is a word in Sanskrit for being out of rhythm, out of sequence, or out of order: *Akrama. Akrama* is inherently disorderly to the point of degenerating into confusion. If you're not going with the flow, with the rhythm you're going against the flow, against the rhythm, against the natural order of the life force. As a Yoga Teacher you want the power of living in tune with natural circadian rhythms. When these rhythms should shape your core habits, your daily self-care behaviors, you have more vitality and resilience to serve. From your centeredness, you can better lead.

If you feel great, and you can guide people to feel good, what you have is in hot demand.

People want exactly what you've got. As a wellness pro you invested time and money consistently in your body wisdom. The people you want to help *have not invested the time and money you have in their body wisdom*. Your body wisdom matters more now than ever.

Watch Cate teach this workshop: yogahealthcoaching.com/toolkit and walk you through the connection between inflammation, habits, and yoga teaching.

Next, let's investigate which habits your students have that are accelerating aging and disease.

What are the 6 Habits Yoga Teachers Shouldn't Have?

As a yoga teacher, it's important for you to realize where your students or clients habits may be the root cause of the inflammation. In my first book, Body Thrive, I walked readers through the daily habits of Yogis. Since 2012, Yoga Teachers in Yoga Health Coaching have guided their students through this habit evolution journey. Together, we've identified the habits that really don't work.

6 Habits Yoga Practitioners Shouldn't Have

1. **Eating a heavy meal later in the day.** Eating heavy foods after the day is done means you are digesting your food during sleep, which leads to poor quality digestion and tissue formation. Eating the biggest meal earlier promotes better digestion, better sleep and better energy the next day.
2. **Being mentally busy or taking in more stimuli in the evening**. The human body circadian rhythm is designed to wind down in the evening. Relaxation, reflection and enjoyment are for the dusk hours.

3. **Going to bed late.** You can tap into the restorative power of sleep before midnight, which engenders being deeply rested the next day. Due to eating late and evening mental stimulation many people have a hard time winding down and sleeping deeply.
4. **Pressing snooze.** Waking early is best for an alert focused mind. When you go to bed late, you either wake up late or don't get a full night sleep. 8 hours of deep sleep is the aim. 100 years ago humans averaged 9, not 8 hours of sleep per night. You see the *akrama*–the pattern that breaks the body and mind down.
5. **Skipping morning exercise.** Movement upon arising is key. First hydration for bowel elimination, and then moving the body to move prana, the life force energy, into the cells. Morning movement with deeper breathing fuels the intelligence of the mind/body/spirit for the day ahead.
6. **Snacking.** Eating between meals disrupts clean digestion. As you age, your body is designed to become more efficient. You require higher quality nutrients in lower quantity. This enables graceful digestion, absorption and elimination of waste. With snacking, a person loses touch with the function of healthy hunger and satiation.

The simple truth that seems impossible to live up to is stated in the Vagbhata Sutrasthana:[1]

> That person who always eats wholesome food, enjoys a regular lifestyle, remains unattached to the objects of the senses, gives and forgives, loves truth, and serves others, is without disease
>
> Vagbhata Sutrasthana

Degenerative habits are negative stressors. The equation is catastrophically predictable:

Poor habits = Negative stressors = Chronic inflammation = Chronic disease = No fun

If you or your students are in this pattern, you can your community on a committed journey into the habits of yogis.

Now, let's look at the hidden costs of these habits.

What Do Your Yoga Students Want: Wealth? Health? Both?

Chronic inflammation has overt costs and hidden costs. Feeling good versus feeling bloated, irritable and tired on a daily basis has quite a cost when you analyze it. The opportunity cost of better health, of mental acuity, of being strong, lithe and fit, and well-rested is real. People like to work with people who are alert, dynamic, vibrant and caring.

Chronic inflammation takes a toll on a person's physical wellbeing–with its drastic impact on digestive health and destruction of healthy gut microbiome, which enables nutrient absorption and waste elimination. With chronic inflammation a person becomes less attractive, and often less confident and naturally at ease in themselves. The effect goes into costs of emotional and mental health.

Mental acuity is sacrificed with chronic inflammation and replaced by brain fog and inability to make hard decisions.

If you, as a yoga teacher, are thinking of what your students of today and tomorrow need, you may be thinking of cracking the code to better daily habits. These better habits are the backbone of the daily routines of yogis for thousands of years. As a teacher, it's a good idea to start to get to know why these smarter habits work.

There isn't much mystery to chronic inflammation from the perspective of yoga and Ayurveda. The yogic precept of self-study, "svadyaya" in sanskrit, points the students awareness into the relationship of making better choices based on experience.

Your Yoga Students Potential to Thrive with the Habits of Yogis

Now, as a wellness pro, you have big choices to make. You can choose to lead your students or clients into their health potential. You can choose to lead to the habits both on and off the mat. The habits rebuild the body's natural intelligence, strengthen digestion, strengthen the mind and restore the experience of inner peace. Plus, their yoga practice will get more fun, easeful, and progressive.

You could lead a journey that awakens your clients potential to thrive. In one year's time your members could be deep into living the regenerative habits - the habits of yogis.

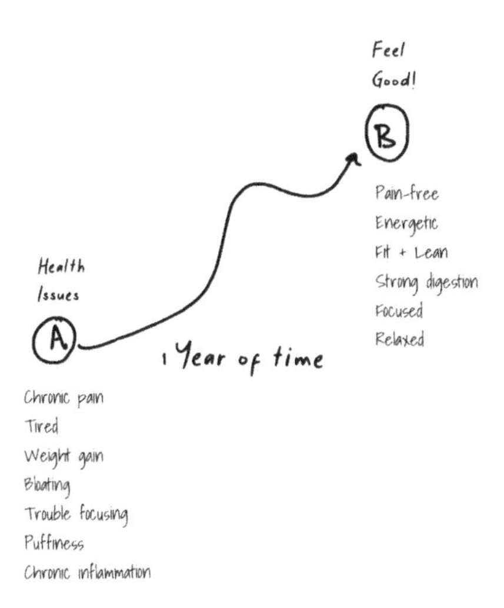

I've found it takes a year to lead for my members to have automated the habits that make them feel good. Therefore the commitment is one year. Time and commitment are the best buddies of lasting transformation. Engage in commitments that leads to results.

My year long group membership program is called BODY THRIVE. At the time of this writing a ticket runs five grand. The habits of yogis are actually free. Exactly none of the habits cost money or are cost-prohibitive. If you have these habits for life you save massive chunks of change. But, more than saving money, members get smarter and more aware of better opportunities. Inflammation costs a person their potential.

COST OF INFLAMMATION

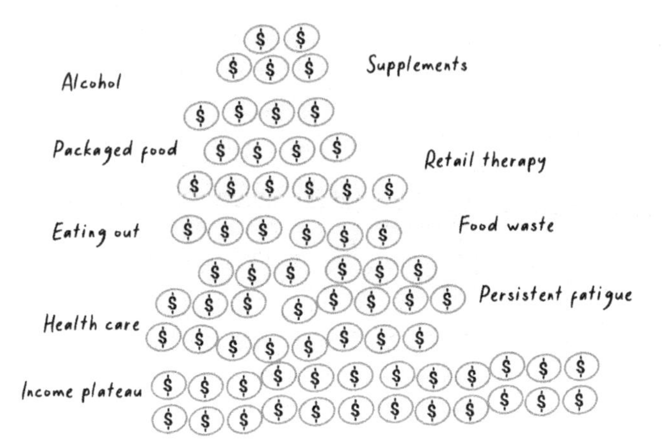

Our members report that their return on investment is exponential, due to how the habits change their future. The habits are equal opportunity habits that general opportunity.

But the five grand. $5000. That's a serious investment. If a yoga students know what the habits are - why would you pay?

They could just buy a book on these habits for $12 on Amazon. They could buy Kate O'Donnell's book on it, or Acharya Shunya's, or Dr. Suhas Kshirsagar's or mine. We all dive deep into the habits of yogis.

If you could buy a book for the price of breakfast, why would you pay $5000 for a journey into the habits of yogis? If a person budgets $100 a week for food - that is their entire annual food budget.

For whom is this a smart investment?

For anyone that is wasting the money. For anyone whose health issues will cost more in the future. For anyone that knows they are wasting their potential.

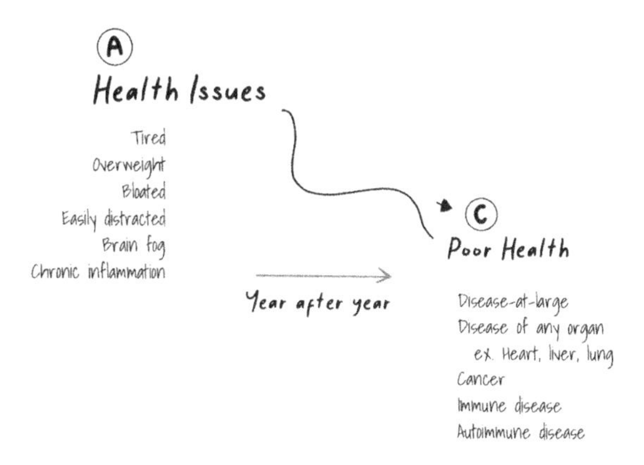

You'd pay because you aren't living the habits. And that is the same for our members. The power of the journey, the community, the focus on results, the success of the past members... that is why members invest in the journey. Before me make this any more about me, let's focus on you.

YOU too can lead the habit evolution journey every yoga student needs right now.

> The alignment of the who and the what are the first step.
>
> Seth Godin

What are the results your members would experience? Well, we have seen so much success, even with beginner yoga coaches. Really, your success will revolve more around your enthusiasm, your care and your ambition. I've run BODY THRIVE as a one year habit journey since

2013. What our members experience is on par with those coached by Yoga Health Coaches. You can see their results from A to B in the image below.

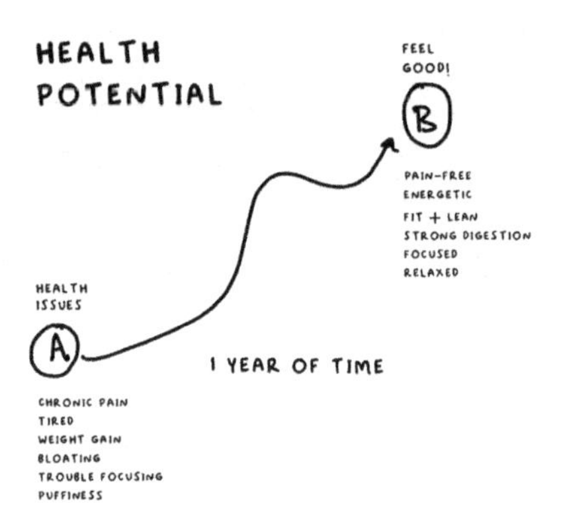

Typical journey members start out bloated, overwhelmed, and has trouble focusing their life and their habits on what matters most and what leads to the experience they want to have. Some are in chronic pain - though sometimes the pain moves from one place to another. In the year they shift from bloated to strong digestion, from flabby to fit, from chronic pain to pain free, from distracted to focused, from overwhelmed to relaxed. The $5k is a good investment for them because their future changes from pain to potential.

The reason I tell you this is because I couldn't guide my students out of their daily habits that generated chronic inflammation with yoga classes alone. To guide them to thrive, I needed to guide a transformational journey. In the next section we'll investigate the actual value of a truly transformational journey.

Pause and ask yourself, what is truly at stake? Time doesn't stop. Habits compound–either towards the positive results of transformation or towards the negative results of accelerated aging and degenerative disease.

p.s. The habits of dina charya are the ancient anti-inflammatory, consciousness-raising, microbiome-enhancing daily habit rhythm of yogis. The foundational teaching is named *dina charya* in Sanskrit. (Sanskrit is the original language of yogis.) Check out BODY THRIVE for all of the fundamental habits.

Transformational Journey vs. Accelerated Aging

For the remainder of this book, we will focus on the value of leading a transformational journey. By definition–it's a journey through time in which the member is guided through a personal transformation. In the wellness industry, the person goes from having health issues, or being in poor health to feeling good.

What's at stake is the opposite journey. The journey deeper into the pain cave, regression, diseased and drugged living. If the student has habits that go *against* the human body's ability to regenerate, to detox, to restore ... then the student will continue to *accelerate their aging* and move on the spectrum towards chronic disease.

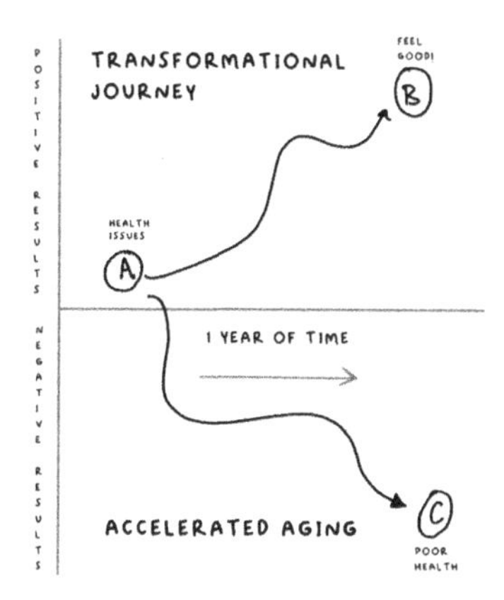

What are the habits that lead one out of health issues into feeling good? Another way of asking is what are the habits of yogis? The habits of *dina charya*?

The Essential Habits of Yoga Teachers & Students:

- Eat an earlier, lighter dinner, to reduce digestive pressure on the body
- Enjoy your evening, offline, and go to bed early
- Wake early, hydrate, eliminate your bowels
- Do breathing and movement before the day begins
- Space your meals–now known as intermittent fasting
- Make seasonal food fresh and daily from local whole foods
- Attune your senses to nature
- Meditate, reflect or sit in silence to clear your mind

If you've ever gone camping without your electronics you might have noticed that you got sleepy earlier. Did you sleep more? Did you enjoy the stars? Did you feel the breeze? Nature restores us back into rhythm.

Now, you don't need to guide yourself and your members to have these habits perfectly dialed in all the time. You need enough of the habits enough of the time to help your body clean up any chronic inflammation and restore a high level quality to your systems and tissues.

As a modern yoga teacher, you may also have chronic systemic inflammation, or a degenerative disease. If you weren't trained in the habits of yogis, it's not too late to start feeling better.

At this point the elephant in the room for any yoga teacher or yoga studio owner usually is their own personal habit integrity. Modern life is full of stressors that bring us away from the natural rhythm of early to bed, early to rise. Modern life is increasingly digital– escorting us away from unadulterated experiences of nature. Being in nature restores us.

Sometimes yoga teachers have what is called "imposter syndrome". Imposter syndrome is where you feel like you are an imposter, rather than the real deal. With the habits of yogis, almost every modern yoga teacher I meet feels like an imposter ... one who may know which habits are better for them, but not able to commit to better habits in their busy life.

Not to worry–we also train yoga teachers in the habits of yogis and show them how to guide both themselves and their students out of the pain cave of chronic inflammation.

Now, let's look at where a transformational journey, such as the journey from feeling tired and bloated to feeling good, lean, and revitalized. Next you'll identify what you stand for as a wellness pro. What are your core convictions?

Your Conviction Leads to Better Results Faster

Now, what we need to do next is get clear on your core beliefs. If you're not in touch with your own core convictions, you don't know your most effective messages to communicate. If you can't communicate effectively, you can't send a beacon to those who are looking for you. And yes, if you have body wisdom and you can communicate you'll find there are people looking for you.

Get clear on your beliefs. After that, you'll see exactly how you can guide the best transformational journey and get paid a premium. And have the time of your life. Like I do. Like I've guided many yoga teachers to do. It's all in the business model. And the model relies on you knowing your core convictions.

Your convictions are what you take a stand for. If you take the time to know your convictions, to write them down, to articulate them, you can speak to your own journey and results *with conviction.* When you speak *with the conviction your results deserve* you open the gate to next level success.

Take a moment to consider.

What are your convictions?

What, specifically, are you willing to make a stand for?

What do you stand for?

What are your convictions for health and wellness?

What are your convictions about health and money?

What are your convictions about your own success?

(Print the Workbook for this worksheet.)

For example, I believe that our habits are communal. That when we're with people with healthier habits we get healthier. When we're with people with degenerative habits, the habits that generate inflammation, it's harder to maintain our edge.

I believe that wellness wisdom is the best long term investment a person can make. I also believe that wellness pros need to a smarter business model to truly lead the journey to health.

I believe that wellness pros who can get results for their clients faster should structure their business to earn a premium. Now, your turn.

Write down your core convictions on health, money, and disease:

- ________________________
- ________________________
- ________________________

Articulating your own journey attracts people looking to experience their own wisdom or healing journey. If you don't speak with your conviction people looking for a solution to their problems won't notice you.

With conviction you need to articulate what is the highest value you can provide. Then you can organize your career around the value of the unique journey you can lead.

Next, we will have a brief lesson in the basic progression of economic value - so that you can articulate the value of a transformational journey. While this pulls straight from Economics 101 - it's a lesson most of us missed.

You already know from the *What You Invested Exercise* what you have valued the most, and where you have invested the most money and time. Now you'll see where your current and potential clients are investing. Remember, people are investing this way, whether it will be with you or with another wellness pro.

I'll also show you the issues and the avoidable issues that arise with Yoga Teachers ready to experience new levels of success. To get the most out of this book, stick around until the end so you get the whole picture and can fast action.

3: High Income Yoga Teachers

How Much Have You Invested Exercise

Look back over the last 10, 20 and for some of you 30 years and do a quick tally of how much money and time you've invested thus far. Use the chart below to write down the line items. Your past investments are your foundation. Include the courses, training, workshops, books, online training, events, plane tickets. Return to the beginning of your journey.

TRAINING	HOURS INVESTED	HOURS INVESTED	WISDOM/SKILLS/ COMPETENCIES

(Print the Workbook for this worksheet.)

Don't skip this step. You can't grow unless you know.

What you just recorded is what differentiates you from the people you are most called to work with.

Now, that you are in touch with your investments and your core convictions, you know your most effective messages to communicate. If you can't communicate effectively, you can't send a beacon to those who are looking for you. If you have body wisdom and you can communicate people looking for results can find you.

Combining your core convictions and your wisdom investments, you'll start to see exactly how you can guide the best transformational journey and get paid a premium. And have the time of your life. Like I do. Like I've guided many yoga teachers to do. It's all in the business model. And the model relies on you knowing your core convictions and best wisdom investments.

Next, we'll look at the economic value ladder so you can see how you've invested in transformational journeys, and how you can help others invest in your guidance through the transformational journey only you can offer

The Value Ladder

Now, let's find out why according to economic theory, the transformational journey earns the most in the marketplace. Yes- that's right. It turns out that the economic value ladder - which is a thing in economics, can explain why you leading transformational journey is the highest value you can offer in the marketplace.

The Y Axis is differentiation of products or services, from undifferentiated to highly differentiated. (I'll show you how to be highly differentiated in today's wellness market.)

The X Axis is price, from low to premium. (I'll also show you what to do to become worth a premium in today's wellness market.)

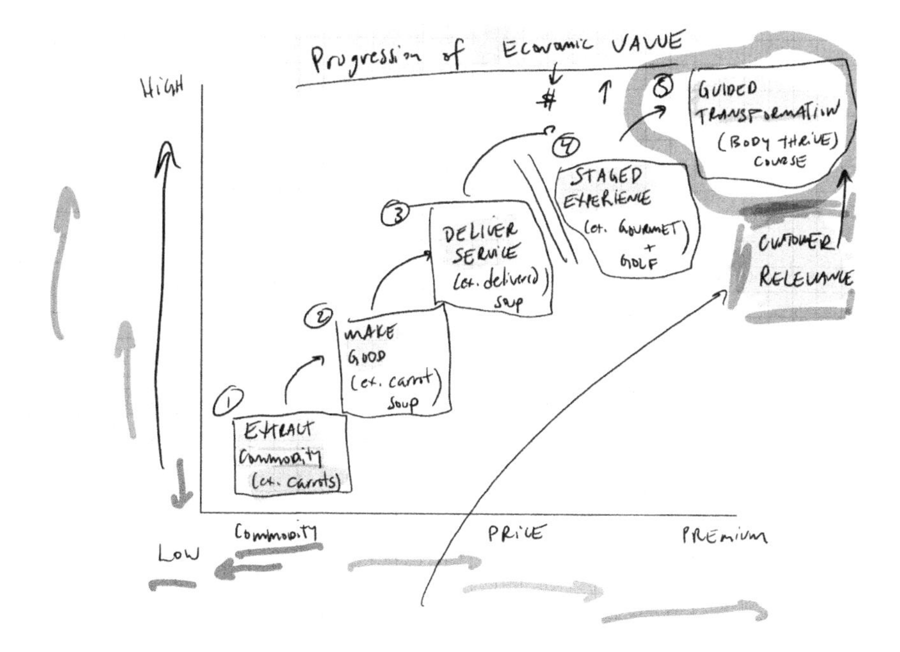

You'll see in the economic value ladder, also known as the Progression of Economic Value, that commodities to goods, to services, to experiences that guided transformation, hold the most value. Humans value personal transformation above all else. See the progression of price from low to premium on the X axis. See the progression of value from low to high on the Y axis. Study this image for a moment, and I'll guide you through each stage.

My hope is that you'll understand that guiding your students through a life-changing transformation, and packaging to that, and selling to that, is your way into a much better lifestyle career.

Humans value

GUIDED transformation

above all else.

The value ladder measures the historical stages of what we value most with our money as humans. It's progressive. There seems to be a natural evolution inherent in our economic progress. That gives me hope. Buckets of hope.

The value ladder is an essential history lesson in economics. I learned this basic lesson from a business mentor that I would pay $1000 a session to coach me as CEO of Yogahealer. I want to pass this onto you for a fraction of the price because I believe that yoga teachers are best suited to guide transformational journeys. If you pay attention, you may benefit as much as I have from taking time to actually understand where your value intersects the modern marketplace.

Let's go through the stages one at a time. As we go, notice the shift from competition to increased freedom in pricing. This has everything to do with your current and future career model.

STAGE 1: Commodities

On the low side of what we value is extracted commodities. For example, carrots. Say you decide to make money selling carrots. You plant and grow them from the seeds you harvested last season. Once you've harvested your carrots you've extracted your commodity and your bring your carrots to the marketplace. You sell them.

Now, if a few other people are selling carrots at the market, a market price is established.

If you charge more than the market price, you probably won't sell any carrots. Commodities are sold at market price because they aren't very differentiated. Your heirloom purple carrots, versus your farmers neighbors heirloom purple carrots aren't going to be different enough to demand a different value at the market. Now, if more people are selling heirloom purple carrots than buyers want at the time, the price also goes down, as you compete with your neighbor for the same limited buyers. Thus, commodities have a low value. Many gym yoga classes fall into the commodity category right now. People compare prices. The market is saturated.

As humans got better at extracting commodities, some people got smart. They realized that for a commodity to be of higher value, it needed to be turned into something of higher value. Now, remember back in human history once upon a time we had fewer goods and services.

Lesson: Money buys basic stuff we need to make other stuff. The more basic–the more competition–the less profit margin.

STAGE 2: Better Goods

People who bought the commodity would often make something with it. Think carrot soup. This making of the goods takes time. If you value time, if time is money for you, you are more willing to pay for the ready made good. With commodities flooding the market, some smart people started to use their time to turn commodities into goods.

When someone came to the market with carrot soup and someone else paid more money than the price of the carrots, the economic progression ladder advanced a rung. Now, say your other neighbor also makes carrot soup. Yours is a carrot potato soup. Theirs is a carrot coconut curry. And you notice that people like her soup more and pay more for it. In fact she has a higher profit margin. You are witnessing how differentiation affects pricing ... and profitability.

Additionally, someone who loves carrot soup, but **doesn't have the time to make it, and has the money to buy it,** is experiencing more value thanks to the evolving marketplace. And that is the second stage. What does this have to do with you earning more?

> If you can help someone on their wellness journey in a way that saves them time you increase your value... and your ability to earn more.

If I can help someone lose 50 pounds in a year *and keep it off for the rest of their life,* it's better than if that takes five years to lose the 50. It's better for the person who has four more years to enjoy the benefits of optimal body mass and optimal energy. They have a new lease on life. Their relationships get better and better.

> How much money is it worth to a person over the next decade to feel good vs. have poor health?

Have you asked? That question is worth asking anyone you could help that is currently not feeling great.

Let's use another example. Chronic pain. Think of someone that has had chronic pain and been on pain medication with side effects for a decade. Say I can help them reduce their pain by 50% and get off the medication, which they want to do, due to the negative side effects. Is it better if we can do that in a year or is it better if that takes us five years? Well, if you're in chronic pain, it's pretty clear that the sooner you are out of pain, the better. We've all experienced that.

Okay, so now we know that time matters.

Lesson: Money buys time. With money, a person will usually choose to get their needs met with greater specificity.

Let's go to the next stage.

STAGE 3: Services

So to review, from #1 to #2, we went from just growing and selling carrots to making something better. Coconut curry carrot soup. Think about it–someone not only planted, grew and harvested the carrots, but they also cooked the soup. Anyone who has money to spare knows what they are willing to pay to have ownership over their time. (And if you enjoy cooking over housecleaning, apply this to the service of housecleaning!) Anyone who knows that time is of the essence in their life will pay more for speed. Stage #3 saves someone even more time by delivering a service.

Not only does your client want carrot soup, but your client doesn't have to go to the market. She can get it delivered.

A friend of mine here where I'm writing from in Alta, Wyoming, had a boutique homemade soup delivery company.

She made the homemade soup and delivered it to her soup club members weekly, throughout the six months of winter. The soup costs more than carrot soup in the grocery store. She used her own recipes. She sourced local organic ingredients. Her soup was of the highest quality (higher economic value) and was delivered (saves more time). Holy cow! What is happening here? Economic value is going from low to high and driving price higher in exchange for time. And you couldn't get soup like hers except from her ... think differentiation.

Pay attention so you can apply this to your wellness career. Pay attention and you'll see the highest rungs of economic value are where you can provide the most unique value–unique to your wisdom and your character–with the most ease.

But, before we get to where your highest value and quickest path to earning more and being of greater value to your clients actually is, you need a solid grasp on stage #4.

STAGE 4: Predictable Experiences

As economies evolved and people had more money *and* more time, they wanted to have very cool experiences. The more the experience met their specific desires, the more they would pay.

In the economic value ladder, this next stage is called Staged Experience.

For example, I was just at my place in Punta Mita, Mexico. An event was happening down the road at the Four Seasons called *Gourmet and Golf.* (I bet you're wondering if they served a spicy cilantro carrot gazpacho paired with a riesling!)

Gourmet and Golf is the epitome of a staged experience. It happens in multiple locations each year. Famous chefs are flown in from all over the world to the Four Seasons gorgeous golf courses. Rich people sign up for a guaranteed fabulous casual tournament experience.

At the end of each hole you have a chef, a dish and a wine pairing. You zoom around in your golf carts with your three other friends. You get a lovely buzz which takes the emphasis off the golf, and onto the fabulous experience itself. The views are divine. The weather is perfect. Your friends are well dressed. The food is exquisite. The wine is well paired. You are *having an experience.*

Later you talk to a friend, who is also loaded and enjoys some casual competitive golf with gourmet pairings. She also threw down her credit card for *Gourmet and Golf.* Her staged experience happened in Carmel, USA, not Punta Mita, Mexico. You compare notes. You compare chefs. You compare experiences, and realize that you more or less enjoyed the same experience. You could each recommend the experience to a third friend and describe it accurately. That is what *Gourmet and Golf* is ultimately aiming for... a reliable product, a predictable experience. So predictable... it seems staged.

How does this apply to you? Your ideal clients may or may not at all be the *Gourmet and Golf* clientele. That is irrelevant. Hippies and Millennials alike through down fat cash for Coachella or Burning Man. Boomers take cruises. Yoga students fly to Bali or Costa Rica to go on a yoga retreat. Bikers rally at Sturgis.

If you are indeed a seasoned Yoga Teacher, you are probably hip to the limitations of staged experiences. Staged experiences feel staged. Take a Disney cruise, for example. Say your extended family wants to celebrate a 60th wedding anniversary. The easiest thing, everyone decides, is to go on the Disney cruise, because of the gaggle of little kids in the family.

When you get back from your cruise your friend who recommended it to you asks you what went down. You compare notes. More than less, you had the same experience that everybody else has on a Disney cruise. Pictures of the grandparents and grandkids with Minnie and Mickey. Pants fitting a little snug due to that ever replenishing buffet table.

Lesson: Staged experiences are well packaged and predictable, yet rarely personal enough to become transformative.

Now, think about this. Recall the Yoga Teacher Trainings you had. Were they staged experiences? Or was there something that was actually quite unique and special so it wasn't staged?

What's the difference?

> The best, most valued personally transformative experiences are tailored to your unique end goals.

As you can see on the sheet here, the next place that it goes, number five, this is the highest. This is where the highest value is exchanged. And, fascinatingly, the most enjoyable and easiest earnings for the wellness professional is to guide invested members through a transformational experience. This will be the most gratifying, creative, and rewarding work of your life.

Drumroll, please ...

STAGE 5: Guided Transformation

Guided Transformation holds the highest value traded in the marketplace today. This is the pinnacle in the global economy throughout history. Pay attention so you can remember this when you are wondering the best way to use your wellness skills. You'll start to see your place in the market from a sharper angle.

> Guided Transformation holds the highest value traded in TODAY's marketplace.

So, what is guided transformation?

Think about your personal yoga journey. Who were your guides? Did you have a teacher? A mentor? A healer? Make a quick list right now. Then, write beside each name, how much you invested in each training or relationship.

Now, make a second list.

List anyone who guided your transformation into becoming a Yoga Teacher. Your teachers, your mentors. The certifications you earned.

How much did you invest to become the Yoga Teacher you are today? Be precise in your re-accounting of your financial and time investment. If you traveled to learn, include that.

For me, I moved across two states to study for two years, to learn and earn two distinct certifications. Once I had my certifications, I then went to India to study with two additional gurus or masters. When I returned to the US, I found two more teachers, one for advanced yoga training, and another for enlightenment and advanced meditation training. Over the years, I've invested $50,000 USD specifically for Yoga Teacher skills. For business skills, I've invested another $80,000. This doesn't include other skills from my undergraduate degree in International Relations and Environmental Politics. All of these investments transformed me into the healer, and the coach and the business owner that I am today. (The undergraduate degree gave me skills in research and writing that helps me write books).

The return on these investments has been 2000%, so I continue to invest more in myself. Remember–it's not the spending that matters ... it's the investing for a return on investment that predicates success. Growth experiences with exceptional guides is the bulk of how I invest in myself. I'm not unusual.

Whatever your investments total, honor the transformation that upleveled you in the process.

Now, back to you. Who are your top three to five guides you've invested the most money with? Look at your notes. You wouldn't know what you know now without that person having guided you through to a higher level of understanding. You wouldn't be who you are today without having had that experience.

Now, take a moment and pause. Reflect. Feel gratitude for these guides in your body. Bow to your best guides for how they helped you develop personally and professionally, based on their wisdom and their experiences.

I hope a lightbulb in your head is turning on. You get to deliver more value. And, you get to receive exponentially more money for your effectiveness in guiding your people and your clients, through a powerful invested transformational journey. You'll bring the best you have to the table.

You will evolve *with* your journey. You will lead by improving your journey for your current and future members. You will innovate as you learn and nurture a unique journey that only you could design and deliver. You get to design this special journey for exactly who you can best help. You get to make it even better than what you experienced in your own journey to thrive.

You get to make it better, to improve upon, to innovate a unique journey that only you could design and deliver.

Remember how the top right part of the economic value ladder goes to premium and also to differentiation? What makes you different from other yoga teachers becomes your differentiation in the marketplace. At the level of transformational experience, you have no competitors. No one can compete because no one will design this transformational journey like you will. What makes you different is now your best advantage.

Because you get to charge a premium at this level, you don't need to work with a ton of people. Exclusivity is built in. Inclusivity is also built in for your members. I'll get deep into premium pricing in the next part, so if you've undervalued your services–stay tuned.

Now, many yoga teachers want to know how to serve the masses, and earn more. The way to do that is to have a free version and a paid version. My free version is my podcast and free workshops. That drives people who actually want to do the journey with me closer towards me, while educating the masses for free.

If you want to earn more, and you don't have a higher price point transformational journey to guide your people through to a better reality, you're doing something wrong. You are making it impossible to earn at a higher level with easier, and better results. That is the beauty about truly understanding and embracing the Value of Economic Progression.

What does this look like? When you lead a transformational journey that people want to be part of, you can charge what the transformation is worth. For many wellness pros looking to earn six figures, a good price point to aim for is about $5000 and guide 20 people. Here is a snapshot of what this might look like, enrolling members quarter by quarter, throughout the year. The rest of this book unpacks how to do just this.

ANNUAL INCOME: 100K

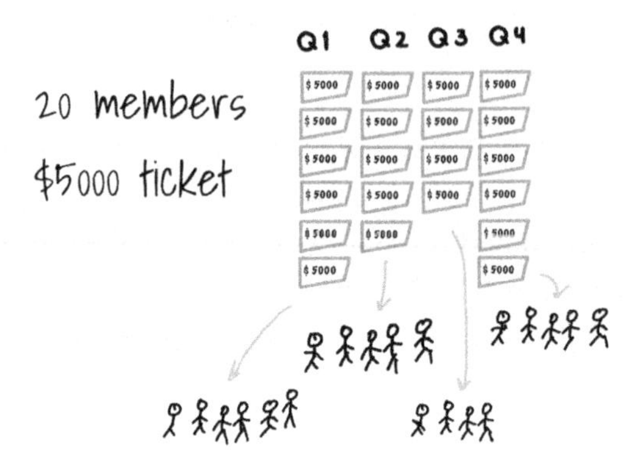

Once you get this, a few issues, or hurdles are essential to build new skills and new behaviors so you can bust your glass ceiling. Let's tackle these one by one so you can earn more faster! The first is packaging, the second is your business model, the third is sales and marketing skills. The good news is that there is an easy way over all three hurdles!

How to Invest in Your Growth

Let's pause and think about how your yoga students *spend* money now. Pause, and also consider how your yoga students *invest* money, including growing their personal wisdom. Consider what is *spending*... versus what is *investing*.

Reflect on how you spend. Reflect on how you invest. Reflect on which of your investments, including investments in growing your personal wisdom, are having the best return on investment (ROI).

Some people consider conventional grocery store vegetables a saving. Others see that as a bad investment. The others don't see organic local vegetables as an extra expense, but rather a good investment. For some, paying a housecleaner is an expense, for others, an investment back into their own time bank account to use for something that has a higher return or a higher value.

In another example, let's look at spending versus investing with business training for entrepreneurs and the self-employed. Like all entrepreneurs, yoga teachers and wellness professionals are self employed or employed by their business. When you work for yourself and want to grow your income you need entrepreneurial and business training, like all other entrepreneurs in the marketplace.

Business training is different than service or modality training. Investing in service training is essential to get the skills to do the service, ex. teaching yoga as a service you offer. To get your company of one to grow and pay your bills and grow your investments, you need business training in addition to service training.

Some entrepreneurs and yoga teachers view their service training and business training as an expense. Yet, successful entrepreneurs view training as an investment. They expect a high return on that investment. Why? Because business training requires their full attention, which means it'll require both a time investment and financial investment on their part.

The second income-multiplying investment obstacle for yoga teachers is differentiating business training from service training. We've found yoga teachers more easily recognize the value, for example, in an Advanced Yoga Therapeutics training, or a Yoga Philosophy Training, then in a training to grow their business. This perspective on investment becomes a stumbling block for most yoga teachers desiring to reach higher planes of financial and career success.

At Yoga Health Coaching (YHC) we train yoga teachers in growing their ability to serve while growing their business. We consistently find the teachers who come to us, having previously invested in business training are the most growth-oriented. Their prior investments in business smarts and service smarts is earning them a better return, which sets them up for more opportunity.

(Visit the Toolkit to watch *How YHC Works Training.*)

If you're good at what you do, and you have the right business model and training, the sky is the limit. In YHC we guide the business model of leading the journey, including the sales and marketing necessary to sell out seats. We guide in how to lead your group, how to lead yourself in integrity with your wellness lifestyle, how to earn through providing deeper value. Many YHC's get up and running in their first six months with us in this model, that could earn them double in half the time with committed, results-invested clients. Our members report the program is an investment with an exponential ROI.

If you want to be financially successful as a yoga teacher, don't view your career training as an expense. Put your money or your earned good credit to the highest return on investment. That is the best place for anyone to put their money. If that investment is you, because you're self-employed, you have an exponential potential, or exponential ROI.

The way I think of it is the more value I can offer the more I should be paid. My focus is on adding value to the market. Right now, my job as CEO of Yogahealer and Yoga Health Coaching is to build a global community by effectively communicating a better vision and strategy for people to thrive in their bodies, in their lives, an in their ecosystems. I write. I speak. I interview. I teach. I generate curriculum. I coach. Overall, I lead.

The more I invest in on-the-job skills, the more successful I'll be at my job. I orient towards the next skills I need to be more effective in adding value by leading the journey for our members and our global community. The better I get at leading the transformational journey - paid members - and leading the global tribe with my vision, my message and my teaching, the better I get at my job. The more money rolls in the door, and the more adaptable my skills are for an unknown future.

My members invest in themselves, through me. Yours will invest in themselves, through you. My members invest in my leadership and step-by-step guidance in their lives. The return on investment is exponential for members because their potential is ignited and in action.

You should do the same. The six figure (*and* seven figure for that matter) business model requires your leadership. Lead the transformational journey. You'll be in better integrity with your own transformation and have a leverageable business model to boot. Not bad.

I've found through over a decade of testing that guiding your people through a one year transformational experience is the best way to lead to results. You'll both need to be committed, invested and results-focused. I'll explain more on the timeline later.

Sometimes, it doesn't seem like humans value transformation above all else, which means the modern marketplace has plenty of room for you to enter the picture. Most people don't know this a transformational experience is something that is possible for them. You, the leader, represent the results. Focus on guiding your people to whatever results you are embodying.

What are we willing to invest in for a premium? How do you best turn your skills into a transformational journey a person can invest in?

If you obsess over this... obsess to lead to the results of the journey... you get to do the most gratifying work of your life. You get to earn as much as you want... because the model is based on results, scarcity (you can't lead that many people after all) and leadership. You get to design your life according to desired results. Win. Win. Win.

If you need to be financially successful, you should understand money and investment.

What humans value with their money and attention follows evolutionary stages.

Economic value–what humans value with their money–follows evolutionary stages. How you spend money and how you spend or invest, reflects what you value the most. The progression of economic value shows how the economy evolves value.

> The more developed we become as individuals the more we are willing to pay for exactly what we want, and spend next to nothing on the rest.

If you stand by your convictions and offer exactly what your people need - transformational results - you can earn a premium.

4: The Holistic Hustle is to Guide the Journey

Why to Package Your Leadership

Now that you understand how valuable your skills are in guiding transformation, you should put your hustle into designing a journey for the people you feel most called to lead. Most often, the first hustle is to build the journey - the journey only you could lead - into a package. Before we get to packaging, let's review.

In order to guide someone through a transformation, they need to be committed to the journey. You need to be committed to guiding them. The start point and end point must be clear. The length of time for the commitment must be concrete. The end goal must be agreed upon. The investment must be a firm reflection of both parties commitment.

Your package must explain:

1. The results-based transformation.
2. Length of time (I recommend a year).
3. How it works.
4. Investment.

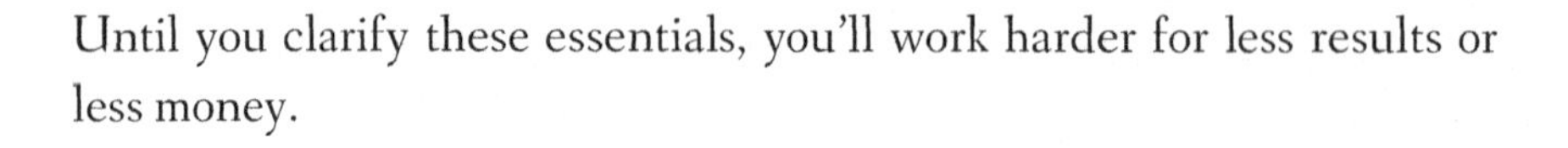

Until you clarify these essentials, you'll work harder for less results or less money.

You can't guide transformation until you package it.

The journey from feeling tired or heavy to feeling great is wrought with challenges. The current habits of your yoga students have serious momentum. This is the momentum of the past. The past has a weight if their habits are degenerative. The past has a lightness if their habits are regenerate.

The downward spiral momentum of degenerative habits present obstacles of formidable proportions. Habits are entrenched in core relationships. If the core people in their life are also in a downward momentum of negative stress, change is even more challenging. Resistance can be strong when a partner, their friends or family have the habits your member needs to uproot to thrive.

Negative stressors are habits that cause stress that results in the body degenerating. Positive stressors, like early morning exercise and intermittent fasting, are habits that cause a positive stress in the body that result in the body regenerating.

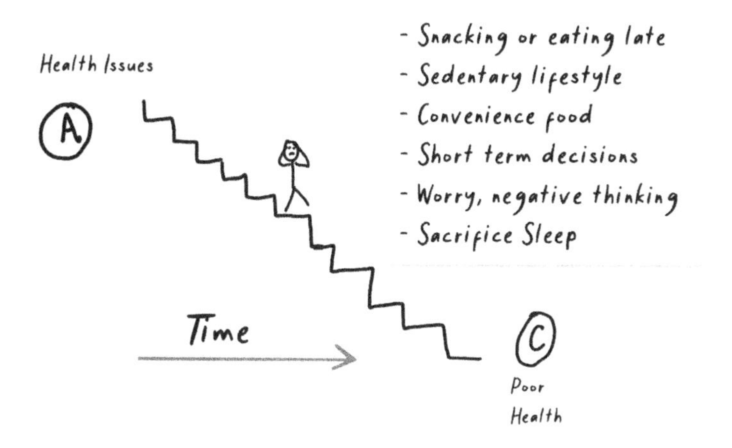

To reiterate... the problem for many of your students is the downhill momentum of the negative stressors in their lives ... and how embedded these habits are in their relationships.

For your students, the momentum of their current habits present obstacles of formidable proportions.

Therefore, the value of a transformational journey is multifold. If you are trained to navigate through the obstacles to success, you can guide your students. The value of an experienced guide, on a major expedition, is usually the main predictor of the expedition's success. Without an experienced guide, the journey is impossible.

Transformational journeys are the stuff vision boards are made of. To get clear on what transformation you could guide, create a vision board. Divide the board in two halves. One half is A. A is the pain points your ideal client currently endures. The other half is B. B is how they could be and feel if you had them committed to your process and your work for a year. A year. A year is a very long time. You have 365 days to guide to results. You have 52 weeks. You have four seasons. What could you do if you were organized? What journey would you guide if you were strategically focused on member results?

(Print the Workbook for this worksheet.)

What journey would you guide if you were strategically focused on member results?

If you are the leader of the journey ... what exactly is the journey you could lead? What results are you aiming for? What would you want the experience to be? Pause and consider. Daydream awhile. Be true to your self, your personality, your unique unicorn-ness. Jot down some notes. The only way this book makes sense is if you take action by thinking, dreaming, and making it real.

How valuable could you be if you nailed the essentials of getting results? Again, which results are you aiming for? Focus on that. As Dan Sullivan of Strategic Coach announced, "We are in the results economy." Which means you can't earn what you should given the wellness skills that you have. Thus, the first hurdle to overcome is to package your transformational journey right for you.

Don't think about enrolling people into your package yet. Focus on designing the package of your guided transformational journey so that you can deliver the most transformation that you're capable of guiding.

Return to the Value Ladder.

The X axis is priced from low prices commodities (like a yoga mat or a pound of turmeric powder) to premium priced transformation. The Y axis represents Differentiation. While a pound of one strain of carrots may differ from another pound, the difference between chronic pain and feeling good are night and day.

What does this mean for you?

The transformation that you can uniquely guide is unlike any other journey. You are no longer "competing" because no one else is you. (This also means you must own who you are and become of increasing orders of integrity with yourself–which we'll get to later.)

> To lead a transformational journey you must own who you are and become of increasing orders of integrity with yourself.

When you can own what you know and prove the value of the transformational journey you can guide, you stop competing on price. Arguably, the value you will now provide is priceless. When you ask someone who was in pain for years and now wakes up feeling like a million bucks what it is worth, they don't say a million bucks. They say the value of their healing transformation is priceless, that it goes beyond words. You should start to break those cost down into specifics.

> Pain, discomfort, excess weight, and brain fog day after day come at a very high cost.

When you package for premium what you're doing has more and more relevance to the people you are guiding. They receive a deep lifelong transformation–which is inherently a lasting return on investment. Design a journey they couldn't get elsewhere. Become more and more relevant to the people that you're working with. As you do, you are increasing your customer relevance by becoming more relevant to your customers. They will want to continue with you and will refer their friends and family.

How to Package Your Journey

Part of the reason I've been a financially thriving yoga teacher for 20 years is because I've always paid close attention to what my people need most. I've designed this next questionnaire for you to become more relevant to the people you want to serve. Here are ten questions you need to answer.

Questions to Package a Transformational Journey

What do the people who you want to work with need the most?

1. What skills do they need to learn?
2. What beliefs do they need to change about themselves and their future?
3. What obstacles are in the way of their transformation?
4. How can you make the most effective and enjoyable wellness journey of their life?
5. How can you save them time?
6. How can you save them money?
7. How can you measure their progress?

8. How long will it take for them to experience transformational results?
9. How long will it take for them to live the habits that lead to those results?

(Print the Workbook for this worksheet.)

If you don't take the time to answer these questions you'll continue to hit your head on a glass ceiling with time, income or impact. You won't be able to guide transformation effectively. Which means you won't earn as much in less time. So, take the time now. Answer the questions. In the process, you'll discover your own relevance to the people you most want to serve.

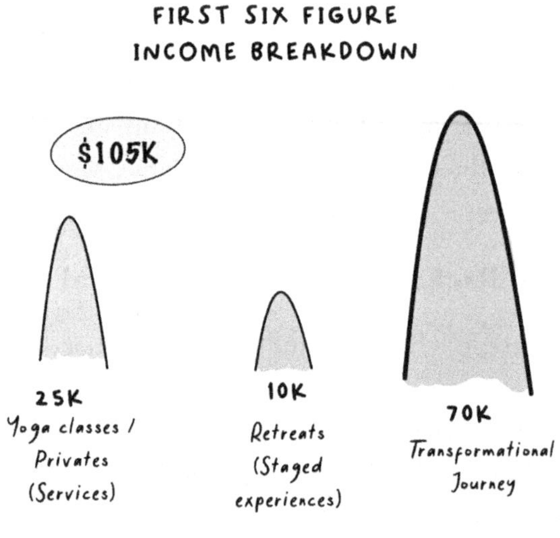

FIRST SIX FIGURE
INCOME BREAKDOWN

$105K

25K
Yoga classes /
Privates
(Services)

10K
Retreats
(Staged
experiences)

70K
Transformational
Journey

You'll also notice how customized and unique of a journey you could guide. Study this chart to understand you are moving from offering services, to offering experiences, to offering a transformation. Each step of the way demands increased customization. Because you don't need to work with the masses, you can go hog wild in your customization, based on how best you can serve your people. Keep in mind–you are evolving from delivering a service to guiding a transformational journey.

Pay close attention to what your people need the most.

Commodities (Extract) > Goods (Make) > Services (Deliver) > Experiences (Stage) > Transformations (Coach)

Reflect on this–you can only guide the journeys you have walked. Who are you a few steps ahead of? For example, due to my training and work experience, I'm qualified to guide a few types of journeys:

- Body Thrive 10 Habits Journey (Body Thrive Course)
- Healing Journey through Ayurveda (Living Ayurveda Course)
- Yoga Teacher Career Success journey (Yoga Health Coaching Certification)
- Live Your True Ambitions Journey (Master of You Course)

The only reason I can guide many journeys is I'm pretty ambitious and built a team to support me. Each journey I guide has earned me over $500,000. Which means I've served my clients to at least that much value. Some of those journeys each earn over $500,000 per year. I've walked those four paths for so long, I know each bend of the trail. I know the specific obstacles that will arise for my specific clients along the way. I know where new members will get stuck, and how to guide them through the obstacles to results. The better you can guide the journey the more relevant you are to your client.

Now, you only need to guide one journey.

You only need to guide one journey to have your best career and lucrative lifestyle.

To help you gain the benefit of my lessons learned along the way I'll give you a brief history of journeys I've offered, what they cost and what I earned, and most importantly, what I learned while I earned. Let's start with lessons from Body Thrive.

Body Thrive is the 10 Habits of Body Thrive from Ayurveda Journey I've guide people through since 2013. When I first offered Body Thrive in 2013, I charged $1250. The journey was 10 weeks for the guided online course community experience. I learned the hard way that ten weeks wasn't long enough for my members to get the kind of results they could get if we had more time. Too much time was spent marketing and enrolling my group every single season! I also learned that the members wanted the group to keep going after the ten weeks was over. The members who re-enrolled became an asset to the newcomers and to the entire experience. In fact, ongoing members were able to see their own progress in context to the new members and more towards the next level of feeling good, while developing leadership skills.

What I learned in those early days, was that the transformational journey for a new member to get the best results from adopting the 10 Habits of Body Thrive, takes **about a year.**

The price for Body Thrive today is $5000 for the year. I enroll more people now than in 2013. The course and dynamic community has always been exclusively online. I do live laser coaching each week with the membership community over recorded sessions. I generated a curriculum and workbook for those that like to learn. I monitor an online forum for answering questions. In the course of a year this is what typically happens:

Quarter 1: The new members join with serious or chronic health issues. The new member learns what the habits of yogis are and how to change their habits with the basics of behavioral science. They become familiar with me and the group. Members connect with an accountability partner. They make progress–sometimes quite quickly. Members also get more honest with themselves and their most degenerative patterns.

Quarter 2: Members are more vulnerable in laser coaching with me, and therefore, can receive 1-1 coaching in our group sessions. Members realize the hard truth about the bigger decisions they need to make right now in their life. The most progressive and meaningful conversations they are having throughout the week are those from the Body Thrive course. They make progress, have better tools, and thrive with the camaraderie in the group to handle setbacks. The member starts to adopt our ethos on incremental change and architecting their environment as they notice how effective this works. They are receiving support and guidance from the group, their guide and focus on automating smarter habits.

POSITIVE STRESSORS

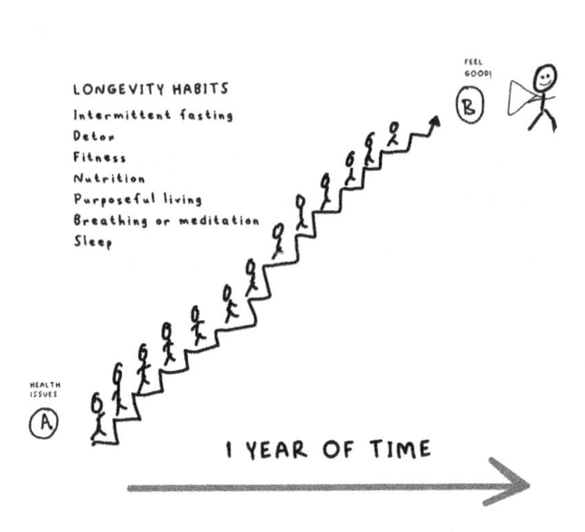

Quarter 3: The member by now has been making tough choices and is gaining momentum in their daily habits. They are living most of the Body Thrive habits most of the time. They have had massive breakthroughs in their health, their energy, their weight and their emotions. Often their addictions are falling away, or becoming too problematic to not face wholeheartedly with the group.

Many of their core relationships at home have pivoted for the better, as they apply what they are learning everywhere in their life. They have growth-oriented friendships with the members in the course. They have been part of the dynamic group and have learned self-leadership skills through our weekly coaching sessions. Members are applying these self-leadership skills in their core relationships.

Quarter 4: The now experienced member is starting to be a voice of leadership to the new members who are just starting. The experienced member can measure their progress in terms of quality of life, and how much money they are saving from better health and feeling great. They want to go into the next course with me to explore their ambition and their potential. Most of the 10 Habits of Body Thrive are automatic parts of their daily routine most of the time. They recognize a massive return on their investment in the course.

Now, if I enroll 20 members per year this generates $100,000 a year of income. If I continue to teach yoga classes that will introduce more people to me for leads for my program. For many yoga teachers, adding the transformational journey is the glass ceiling breaker in their career.

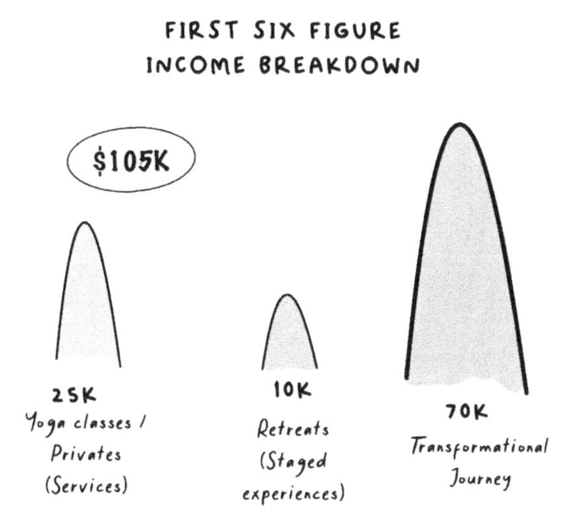

Now, the beauty of the transformational journey is that you can scale it if you want to. I find that most of the yoga teachers I work with in Yoga Health Coaching are happy around the six figure mark, maybe up to $150,000 USD a year. After that, they are comfortable and don't want to work more or add complexity. Many of our Yoga Health Coaches drop a few yoga classes in desire to work with their more committed members. With multiple income streams, there are many choices. One example of where this career path goes is in the image below. This is an advanced YHC member, who has also added an advanced tier–a paid

Mastermind group to their echelon of offerings. Most teachers I know aren't this ambitious. I am, and for others like me, I'll include the details.

MULTIPLE SIX FIGURE INCOME BREAKDOWN

$300K

20K
YOGA
CLASSES
(SERVICES)

10K
RETREATS
(STAGED
EXPERIENCES)

200K
TRANSFORMATIONAL
JOURNEY

70K
VIP /
MASTERMIND

The multiple six figure income requires a techie virtual assistant, usually to help with social media and customer service. However, the investment in team enables the teacher to do their best work–which is working with members and enrolling future members. (We'll get to enrollment in a hot minute).

Now, at Yogahealer, we use the same model to guide transformational journeys between the price points of $5000 - $15000. You might wonder where we find people who want to invest this kind of money in themselves. Surprisingly, it's not the wealthy. It's people like you and me. People who want to invest in themselves, in their body wisdom, in their better, smarter future. Most people get that they are their own best investment ... especially when things start to break down.

Most Yoga Health Coaches start out by leading small groups of 10-30 people. I prefer big groups. I always have. I've always wanted to make a big impact and bigger groups work well for me. Now, most Yoga Health Coaches prefer to work with smaller groups. You get to choose what you want to lead, and what you want to do with your group. Taking ownership of your personal preferences is part of designing your career and your life as well as the journey you are leading.

Now, we tend to have over 50 members a year in Body Thrive. The members like feeling the momentum and interconnectivity of our global community. They also like the experience of being with people from around the world that are also striving for better everyday. We use better leadership tactics so that all benefit from every live coaching sessions. Dynamic groups is part of our training for Yoga Health Coaches to learn this skill.

Members are empowered by the spirit, the ethos, and the deep honesty the group provides. They like the flexibility of being online. They don't waste time coming and going, and they can access the conversation no matter their travel or work schedule.

How Long is a Transformational Journey?

I've tested ten weeks, I've tested three weeks, I've tested twelve weeks, I've tested six months, I've tested two years. I have found that one year makes all the difference. A full cycle around the sun, a spin through the seasons, a complete turn of the wheel of life is required.

I've found a few reasons for this:

1. People need time to transform.
2. Trust is built over time.
3. Each season brings up different challenges and breakthroughs.

People need a full year to give the space and time for their deepest challenges. These challenges surface with time. If you don't have enough time you'll witness the cycle of progression followed by regression. Guided transformation is life-changing when there is vulnerability with the leader and the group. Vulnerability relies on trust. Trust takes time for development.

Also, I find most members start the course in a rush. Most come into their membership overwhelmed. Having a time container of a year helps people relax and slow down. This paradox of slowing down and making small steady improvements leads to more rapid and lasting results. To thrive faster, more efficiently, we have to be relaxed and present with ourselves.

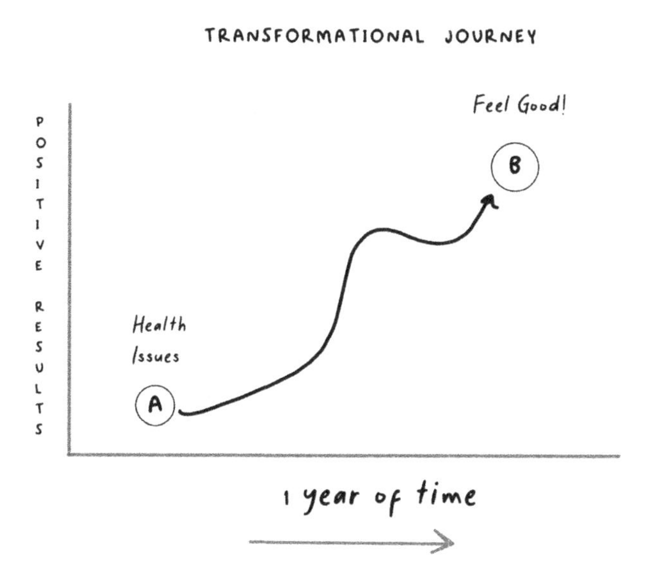

Now, the Yoga Health Coaching journey I lead has grown into two years. I used to offer this as a year, with the option to join the second year. However, I found that the members who invested in two years upfront had better results. They liked having a commitment of steady guidance for the career changes they needed to make in their wellness careers to double or triple their income. They were more committed to the methods, to building systems, and leading with their lifestyle. Plus, they developed a network of colleagues that were using the same methods. Again, based on results, I changed the length of time to two years. Many recommitted for a third year to continue to have access to the growth community.

How long will it take your members to get results, to have breakdowns of old patterns and to stabilize breakthroughs of new habits? That is how long your journey should be. Don't underestimate the power of a community of belonging and becoming.

Your Zone of Genius

Zone of genius is a term from Gay Hendrix in his book The Big Leap. While we can all spend time working in our zone of excellence, or where we have the skills to excel, the best work of your life is to be found in your zone of genius. We'll look at two ways for you to learn more about your zone of genius. Let's start with your Wealth Dynamic.

Wealth Dynamics is a personality test that I've found extremely helpful in working with yoga teachers. You can take it online for about $100 investment. Unless you've already taken a battery of personality tests to point out how it's easiest for you to build wealth in your yoga career you should invest in this test.

Through my members in Yoga Health Coaching I've discovered most yoga teachers fall into a mix of four of the eight categories–supporter, star, creator or mechanic. Why is this important?

The better you can articulate your personality along with your expertise, the better you can articulate how you naturally lead to results. Own the experience members will have on your journey.

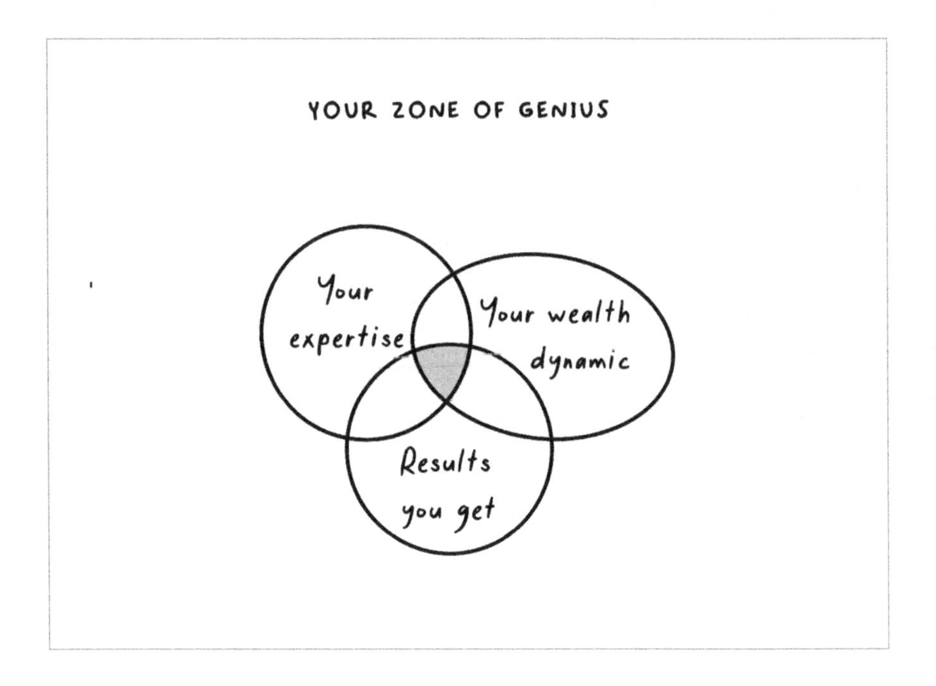

I've taken a half dozen personality tests. I always come out on the creator or innovator category. This makes sense as I was precious in leading journeys through Ayurveda, precocious in starting Yogahealer.com during the dot.com bust of 2000, precocious in podcasting, precocious in bringing all of my courses online by 2012.

I didn't realize I was precocious.

Once I took the test I discovered my Wealth Dynamic is creator/star. I like to create things–like multiple journeys! The star in my Wealth Dynamic enjoys being on stage, grabbing the mic, leading big groups, and growing a global thriving community.

Many yoga teachers are good mechanics or good supporters. These personality-driven skills are two entirely experiences for members. I love the wellness professionals in my life who excel in body mechanics. They can identify the root of my pattern and guide me to unwind it or some can unwind it through working directly on my body. You want a good mechanic. Supporters are entirely different. Supporters build a network of support around a member that is changing, is evolving, or is struggling to handle pain. Without support, the member can isolate and regress.

The point is, if you know your wealth dynamic, you can articulate how you guide members to results in your transformational journey. You'll operate in your zone of genius.

Now, before you lead a transformational journey, you won't know what results you will get. However, you can look back at the work you've done thus far. What are the trends in your personality over time? What do your students say about the results they've had since working with you?

If you haven't asked, now is the time. You want to know the results of your work. You want to understand the value, the savings to that person, the new opportunities in their life, and how their life has changed as a result of your work together. You want to learn your student's stories, and soon, your members stories. You want to be able to vocalize and repeat these stories to those who haven't worked with you ... yet.

Positive Stressors

The journey I guide Yoga Health Coaches to lead is to change negative stressors into positive stressors. We guide people to the longevity habits, long ago codified by yoga. These habits are the endangered habits of our species.

Yet, interestingly, they are relatively easy to adopt in a group. The group must already have the habits in momentum. That is the key, and it's a key in your transformational journey. In Yoga Health Coaching we show how to build a membership community where experienced members support new members. This is the fastest way for new members to evolve, and experienced members to evolve in leadership. Of course, when you're starting out this is impossible. However, building with the end in mind is the much faster path to success.

I've already identified that the positive stressors we guide our members to automate as habits include intermittent fasting and fitness and breathing exercises. Living a life of purpose of meaning is also a positive stressor. Our members gain momentum with meaning in the second half of their year long journey. This is a natural outgrowth of better daily habits that emphasize being a well rested, well nourished, relaxed and focused human being. Another positive stressor we use is detoxing. I've found seasonal detoxing to be a fundamental, a necessity, for detoxing chronic inflammation from the body and a faster path to shift outdated mental and personality habits.

What I want you to notice from the image below are the people on the staircase. The staircase starts at Health Issues and ascends to Feeling Good. Our existing members create a forward momentum for new members. This momentum is group generated. Meaning momentum is not reliant on me exclusively as the leader or on any other member. Every member has access to this momentum all the time. Even me. And some days, I can really use the group's momentum to engage in the positive stressors that result in feeling good!

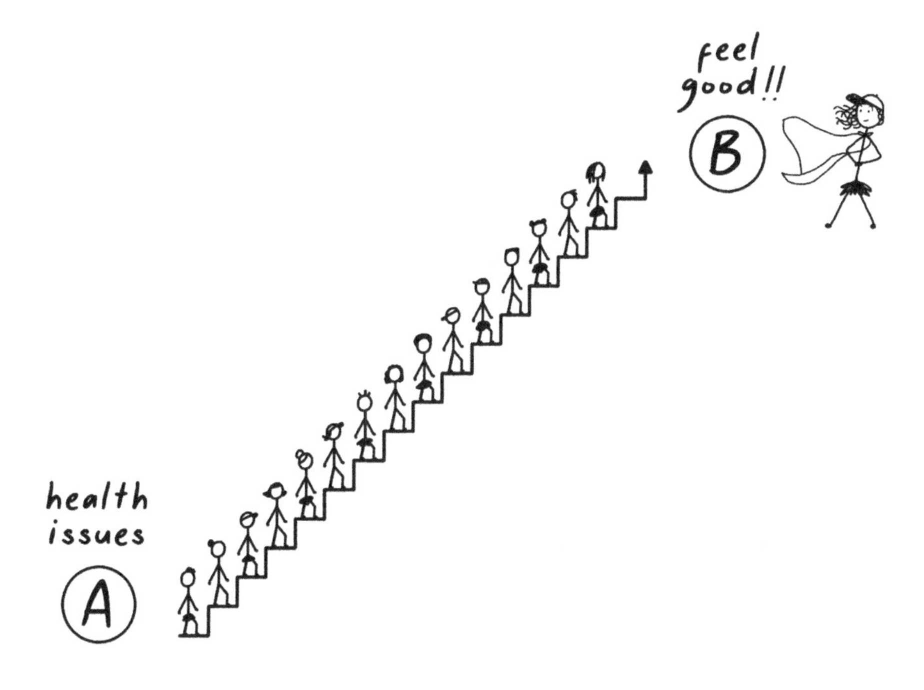

What is in Your High Ticket Item?

Now that we've been talking about positive stressors and group dynamics, you get to update what you want to include in your transformational journey.

I've focused on the habits and the results. I haven't focused on "how" I guide members to results.

Like most online teachers, I use a combination of video trainings, live coaching sessions, worksheets and a forum. I have an online course hub I've developed over the years.[1]

You may have video trainings, online sessions, in person sessions, live events or meetups, retreats, guest teachers and curated experiences. Let your imagination run wild. Some of the yoga teachers I've trained incorporate garden parties, wild plant walks, art therapy workshops, fridge overhauls. What would get your client to results? What would enhance the journey?

Record what you will include in your journey:

____

________________________________ ________________________________

____

____

________________________________ ________________________________

____

____

________________________________ ________________________________

____

____

____

(Print the Workbook for this worksheet.)

Price your Ticket

Now, you might be wondering what your ticket price should be. You want to price your journey based on the transformational results you can guide.

In the last section, I asked you to ask your yoga students what results they have had since working with you. Write out the answers to these questions now. Then, if you haven't already talked to your students, add their feedback as well.

- Which clients had the best results from working with me?
- What were those results?
- What were those results worth?
- Could I get someone like them to result faster now that I have more experience?
- What are the additional benefits my client experienced from those results?
- How much money were those results worth to that client?

Once you answer those questions you'll have a ballpark number for the value of your journey. Value should exceed price.

Next, write down what you want is in the package of your transformational journey.

Write down the ballpark price for your Transformational Journey:

One guideline on pricing I respect is from Dan Sullivan from Strategic Coach. Dan recommends going with the price that scares you and then adding 20%. The reason for adding the 20%?

> The added 20 percent is your commitment to yourself, your commitment to your value, and the proof that you're willing to go through a period of courage that might include rejection because you want to develop a new capability and be better paid for how good you think you'll be in the future.
>
> Dan Sullivan, Strategic Coach

You want to price your membership to deliver a return on investment that is exponentially higher than the investment. And, you too should want to develop a new capability or capacity for you good you could get.

While your price depends on your level of experience in guiding people to results there are also other factors. I've found with many yoga teachers I've coached, the leadership personality they've chosen to develop matters as much as their level of experience.

Someone with natural self-confidence and a strong ability to connect with people can easily charge more than someone who is shy and withdrawn, regardless of skill. Now, personality is shaped by habit.

Meaning, with new habits that focus on confidence and connection, a yoga teacher can dramatically improve their earning potential.

> A yoga teacher can dramatically improve their earning potential by focusing on connection and results. Confidence is built by experience.

Now, confidence in your communication is built like any other skill. Communication capabilities are most critical when industry turbulence is high. And right now, industry turbulence is very high.

To improve your communication follow this advice:

- Consistently and authentically communicate your care.
- Challenging yourself to achieve at higher levels.
- Grow beyond your previous potential.
- Effectively communicate your achievement.
- Witness your confidence soar.

SIGNS YOU ARE PRICED TOO LOW

You need to challenge yourself to charge what the transformation is actually worth. When you challenge yourself you will get rejections. If you hold to your vision you will also get clients with significant skin in the game. The price point must be high enough for this to be a serious decision, with full commitment. Remember, the cost of degenerative habits is poor health. Poor health is always more expensive in the long run.

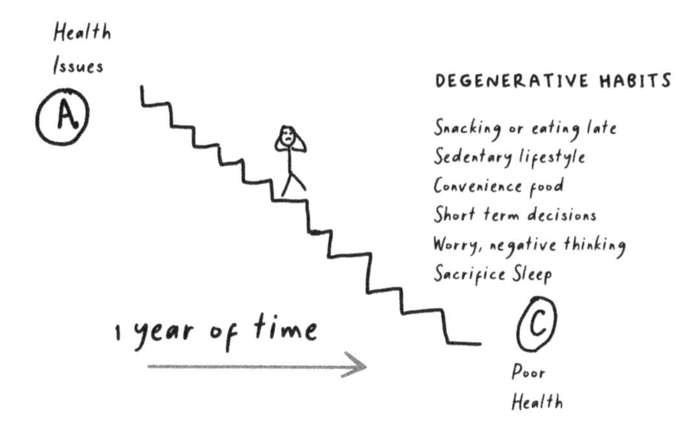

Have you ever heard someone complain about the rising price of groceries and then drop $150 at a fancy restaurant? Or drive away from class in a luxury car? People are often irrational with money and spend on what they value.

Skin in the game

As a competitive soccer and basketball player I was taught to have skin in the game. More often then not I left skin on the field or on the court. Skin in the game is referred to in psychology and economics as "escalation of commitment." Skin in the game is a sunk cost on the way to return on investment.

The hard choice for people to part with their money happens during an enrollment process. Once invested, people don't want to lose their investment. This creates an effect where if you can get people ready to invest in themselves, once they do, they'll be relieved.

> Once invested, the person's identity and complete orientation toward their objective changes. Because they now must go forward, they're no longer confused about what they need to do. They've already acted, and now they need to make good on that action.[1]

Without skin in the game, you can't get members to results. If your price isn't high enough you won't get committed members.

Yoga teachers set their prices too low because they don't want to learn how to do sales. Enrolling your members is sales. We'll get to sales in a bit. Right now, you need to think how much skin in the game do you want from your members?

How big are the results you are willing to guide to?

Your price needs to reflect your desire to show up with your best 100% of the time. With sales skills, which are learnable, you will also get clients investing at a higher level.

The more your members are invested, the more value can be exchanged in your journey. On average, the Yoga Teachers I coach, want to guide about 30 people per year through a transformational journey. They charge a range $2000 - $12000. The difference in price reflects (a) their experience and (b) their confidence.

> The more your members are invested the more valuable your journey will become.

If we return to the Economic Value Ladder from earlier, there is a third dimension to how people spend money. This third dimension is a plane called Velocity of Relationship. Velocity of relationship reflects the speed of commitment and trust. I've seen new members gain traction towards feeling good very quickly, members who I met for the first time in the enrollment process just weeks before. The speed in which we gained trust in working together had everything to do with knowing what results they were here to get with me and them having skin in the game.

If you understand this you will be able to get to work with people who are looking for results now, and quickly. You'll be able to work with people at premium pricing. You'll be called to do the best work of your life.

Developing the Leader Within You

I bet you're wondering how to find 20 people to enroll at $5K a pop, or maybe you already tried and failed. Now, before you put the cart before the horse, let me stop you.

Just think ... if you did, it would look like this:

We've had new members of Yoga Health Coaches do this in their first three months of YHC training. However, it's not the norm. More yoga teachers who start with us have issues with confidence, are slower to take action, and aren't ready to engage in the process with no holds barred.

Yet, even the slower starters get the hang of getting their pilot off the ground.

What is a pilot you ask?

A pilot is a small enough group to gain momentum moving from A (Health Issues) to B (Feeling Good). You don't need all 20 to begin. Seven is a fine number.

What is important is that you get your group going. What is next most important is that you get invested members. If your members aren't invested in results, you'll all struggle with commitment. Remember–a year is a long haul. A year is a playground for transformation. For your pilot to gain traction you want invested members and personal endurance.

Converting interested prospects into members is a sales skill. Decide to kill it at sales, and guided transformational journeys are your oyster.

PILOT GROUP

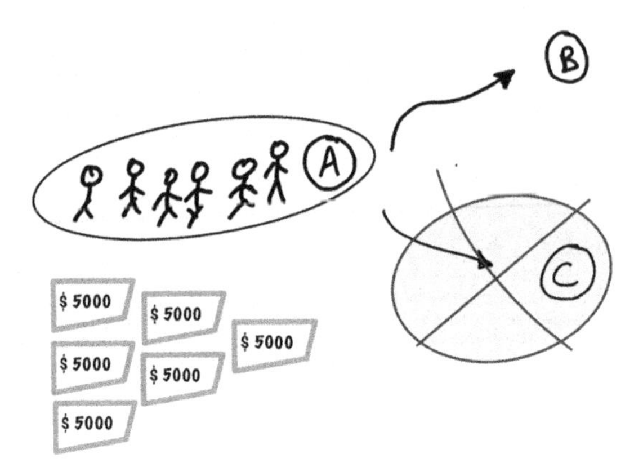

We find it takes a month or two for people to get their pilot enrolled. Then, it's a matter of building a system around enrollment. If your group goal for the year is 20 people at \$5k, and your focused on enrolling 1.6 people a month, you might allow new members to start quarterly or monthly. Often new journey coaches are shocked to hear that their group will fair better and members will gain traction faster with rolling enrollment.

ANNUAL INCOME: 100K

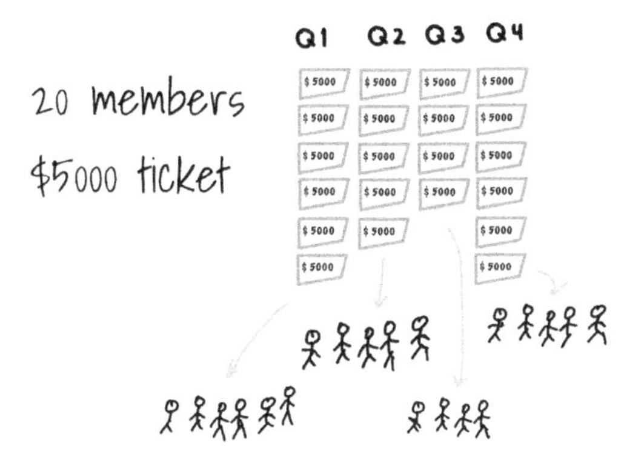

At Yogahealer and Yoga Health Coaching we've tested quarterly and monthly enrollment for a decade. What we've found is that it works. The group grows as members want their friends to come on the journey and as you convey the results happening within your group. As members get results, they see their progress in the new members joining. Also, many experienced members meet their new best friends as the group expands. People don't come to the group to meet their best friends; it's simply one of the many side benefits of having skin in the game in a guided transformation.

The Big Surprise in Leading Your Community

The craziest thing about leading a journey to results... which is our business model behind Yogahealer, Yoga Health Coaching, Body Thrive and even Master of You... is that the journey leads turns around and leads you.

When you lead a community the community starts to develop the leader within you. The circle of leadership only moves forward when one chooses to lead.. and listen.

I've been leading journeys for twenty years. Leading journeys to results made me rich and free, and steered into becoming the leader I'm meant to be. I've seen this time and again with this smarter community leadership-based business model.

5: Break the Yoga Income Glass Ceiling

What about Impact vs. Income?

> The amount of money someone is willing to pay you will be in direct proportion to the amount of confidence they have in your ability to get them results.
>
> Marketing Expert Diego Rodriguez

At this point most Yoga Teachers realize a few things.

1. You don't need to work with more than 20 people a year at the $5k price point to have a six figure income.
2. You aren't sure how many people you want to work with per year.
3. You really aren't sure how much money you actually want to make.
4. You got into being a yoga teacher for the impact more than the income.

All of these realizations are important to acknowledge. I've had all of these realizations myself at multiple points in my career. Back in 2002 I offered weeklong private 1-1 retreats. The price tag I charged was $3500 per person. That was twenty years ago, and I was fairly green if you know what I mean.

I was just starting out as a Yoga Teacher and Ayurvedic practitioner. In 2002, I worked with a client and her family for two weeks. I walked away with a check for $13,000. I had never imagined I could earn that much money that quickly. The client valued the experience so much, she invited me back to give her five additional private retreats that year. I worked with her in this way for the next decade. She had friends that also wanted to work with me. That is what happens when the results speak for themselves.

Yet, I also had reservations about working for wealthy families. I realized I wanted to also have a big impact with my work. I wanted to work with hundreds of people. I wanted to influence thousands of people. I wanted millions of people to experience thrive due to my impact. I wanted to be part of the solution. I wanted to stop the madness, the snacking, the high quantity low quality lifestyle that kills the human spirit. I wanted many people to experience lifelong vibrant health.

Truly, I've always felt that a global positive impact was possible with a life devoted to a specific mission. What I'll show you next is for those who want to make a difference. A big difference.

First, remember, this is entirely optional. You could work with 10-30 people a year. For example, in the high performance, peak performance niche. This niche has successful people with access to resources and usually a voice in their field. I work with many Yoga Teacher as YHC members who are deeply relieved to know that it's okay to focus on small. If you play on the smaller side of groups, you can offer a boutique or VIP experience for your members like I used to. Many part time Yoga Teachers are relieved to think of having a small group–even 10 people per year in their transformational journey. They can work very part time, from home or locally, or globally, and still earn higher than the nation's average median full-time income.

If you're thinking "*My work, my dharma, is bigger than working with 10 to 40 people a year*", I get that.

Think of impact as that which you can do for free using the megaphone of social media, podcasting, video tutorials or talk shows, blogging and book writing. Most of these activities are challenging to monetize in a way that the pennies add up to retirement investments. You can choose to do these activities to bring you a steady stream of members for your transformational journey. But, let's not confuse things. There are easier ways to attract members than devoting a chunk of your time to impact the masses.

I speak from years of experience. I started building my email list in 2001. I was just trying to keep in touch with my workshop attendees, yoga students and Ayurveda clients in an organized way. I didn't even know it was called list building. Later, I started blogging so that I wouldn't have to type answers to my students and clients frequently asked questions. I would send out the link to the blog post instead. By 2012 I had generated an archive of audio interviews with famous yoga teachers and Ayurvedic gurus. My friend begged me to put them on the web, so I put all the files into a podcast. That kicked off the Yogahealer podcast. Since 2012, I've rarely missed a week. I added an additional show for the Yoga Health Coaches to communicate as a global community. I have hired a team of people to edit audios and post clips to social media.

This is all impact work. Yes, this work helps us attract the right people to become members. And if you want to build a personal brand or a company based on impact, you too may decide to have a much bigger social presence.

Now, one way to know if you are seriously driven by impact is to measure your impact. Below are examples above on how I measure impact. It's not a brag. Honestly, I would have thought I would have had a greater impact for how long I've been in business at Yogahealer.com. I sense the bigger impact is coming in my future. Publishing books like this are part of the effort to guide more yoga teachers to do their best work yet. And honestly, 20 years ago I never would have guessed at the wealth I've been able to generate for my family while having a freedom lifestyle and a small online team.

For years I've averaged about 30,000 downloads a month on my podcast. I have at any given time around 80,000 people on my email list. I've written a few books that have sold maybe 15,000 copies. Facebook tells me I have 5000 friends and 60000 fans. I know how many people I'm actually influencing. Our IG account is growing, and we just started Cate Stillman playlists on Youtube to offer more people free training.

Notice that I measure.
I have a strategy for influence.
It's work and for my lifestyle requires a team.

If I didn't care about influence or global evolution, and I just wanted a lifestyle career–I wouldn't bother.

I'm also crystal clear on my time investment for impact with those who get me for free or close to free via a podcast, books, newsletters with tip sheets, and social media lives. This isn't the same ballpark as those who pay a premium to be with me live in laser coaching. For those that want access to my sacred, dynamic community of colleagues, they need to have skin in the game. That way, I can increase my attention and my care that they get to specific end results.

So, if you want to make a big difference, and earning more is very important to you right now, I recommend thinking about it like this: think about your income and your impact separately. Look at income as your business to supply your financial needs, desires and future investments, including your impact investments. A high quality life isn't cheap. And cheap isn't the point. Living your best life is the point. If you need to earn more to make that happen, good. I'm teaching you how to earn more. In earning more you increase your skills, your capacities, your value as a dynamic, powerful human being.

A reminder: to be clear, *if you're not wanting to work more*, if what you actually want is a lucrative lifestyle, you might decide to devote or tithe 10% of your working time to impact. The rest, you might focus on your members.

You + Your Group's Potential

For the yoga teachers who join me for guidance in leading the journey–who enroll in Yoga Health Coaching–there are a few skills gaps. The reason they invest is to close those gaps fast and get on to earning more by doing the best work of their lives. When they close those gaps the immediate effect is a return on their tuition investment with me.

What are the gaps?
Packaging.
Sales.
Dynamic group leadership.
You started on the packaging. I'll get to the sales in a minute.

If you study the image below you'll notice categorical crossovers in how you lead and how you guide. Most teachers are good teachers. Teaching isn't the same as guiding a group to results. Quite a few of the teachers I've worked with have had an identity crisis over dropping the habit of teaching.

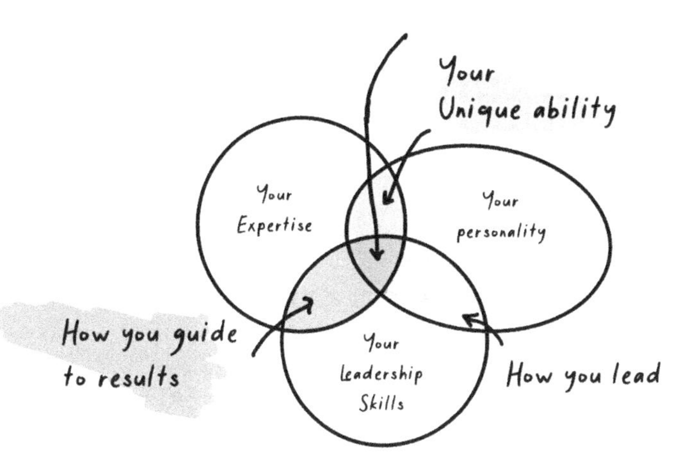

Teaching is hierarchical in the way that the teacher teaches the students. The students are subordinate to the teacher. In a dynamic group, the leader must lead. Developing your style of leadership will play off your wealth dynamic.

Education is the kindling of a flame, not the filling of a vessel.

Socrates

Peak Performance in the Results Economy

When you're getting great results for your members, and you're getting results faster, you will need to raise the price to get even better results.

As you get better at what you do, you naturally want people to have more skin in the game. Whenever you notice your clients aren't committed to getting results, your pricing isn't high enough.

> We are in the results economy.
>
> Dan Sullivan Strategic Coach

I raise my prices whenever I feel like I'm over delivering and under-appreciated. Whenever I notice that people aren't taking full advantage of the offering, which could be demonstrated by not showing up on time, not showing up with questions, not taking action between sessions, I raise my rates.

What I find most frequently is that they are not focused on getting their clients to results. Often, they can't articulate what results they can guarantee if someone does the work of working with them wholeheartedly. They haven't built the habit of results-based communication. They haven't taken the time to find out what their students actually want from working with them. They haven't built a results-based journey. All or any of these scenarios will keep a glass ceiling over your head.

> What results could you guarantee if someone became a member on your journey wholeheartedly?

These same Yoga Teachers complain about how their students are not consistent, or not committed, or not progressing. All of these issues reflect time for money pricing, not results-based pricing.

You should aim to become increasingly skilled at what you do. You should aim to charge a premium for your services. As you improve in your skill year over year you increase the value you are able to exchange with your clients. If your pricing doesn't reflect this increase in value, your clients won't actually be able to receive at the level you are able to give. And that is an avoidable shame.

> Both the career model and sales problem yoga teachers face are solvable with specific skills.

Where are your Future Clients Now?

Once you embrace the transformational journey, you may wonder a few things. Where will your journey members come from? What will be their objections to enrolling? How will I get their attention?

First, let's get clear on how many members you will want to enroll per year and then break it down per month.

1. How much money do you think you should make in the next year if you were guiding members to results? ____________

2. How many people do you want to guide per year? ___________

3. Divide how much you should make by the number of people ____________. This is the cost of your transformational journey. (Your other income streams can be used to help you build your career.)

4. Divide the # of people by 12.____________

This is the number of people you need to enroll per month. For example: $/year = $100,000

1. People/Year = 20

2. Journey Cost = $5000
3. # Enroll per Month = 1.6

So, your enrollment number is 1.6 people per month. Month after month. Like I said earlier, you can have a very lovely lifestyle working with 20 people a year. If your cost of living is just $60k a year, you could invest $40k per year. Not bad long term planning!

In this example, you'll need to attract maybe five good leads per month in order to enroll the best two qualified people for you to escort on your year long journey of transformation.

Now, remember that the top number–your total income–is scalable with this business model. In the pricing section I talked about increasing your prices as you increase your skills. As your transformational group gains traction, you may decide to increase your price, say to $8500.

If that sounds outrageous to you, do you know that other yoga teachers are earning this for guiding people to results? They are enjoying their work because their people are financially committed. Everyone they work with has skin in the game!

You won't need to work with more people to make significantly more money. Or you may decide, over time, you want to double the people you bring on your transformational journey, and just raise your price to $7500. You would then earn $300,000. Same business model with a bigger group and a more experienced transformational journey. So, as you can see, these numbers are flexible. The important thing for you now is to focus on your right numbers as you build your skills.

I know of people who work with 10 people for $25k. It's an elegant $250k income. If you are a highly skilled body mechanic and can lead to results that are worth more than $25k a year to someone, and you want a lifestyle career, why not?

> Price yourself at enough of a stretch that you'll show up with all you've got and continually improve.

Why make your life more complicated?

Now, if you are just starting out as a Yoga Teacher, and you don't have much experience or much confidence, I have a few pieces of sage wisdom.

1. Work with people you know you can help.
2. Price yourself at enough of a stretch that you'll show up with all you've got and continually improve.
3. Raise your rates as your value increases.
4. If you are already ace at what you do, acknowledge that time-earned accomplishment in every cell of your being. Build your sales skills, and read on.

Your Leadership Development Program

Your potential is tied to your groups potential. Your groups potential is only limited by your ability to lead. Your group will demand your leadership. Which means your unique skills reliant on your unique ability, how you lead, and how you guide to results.

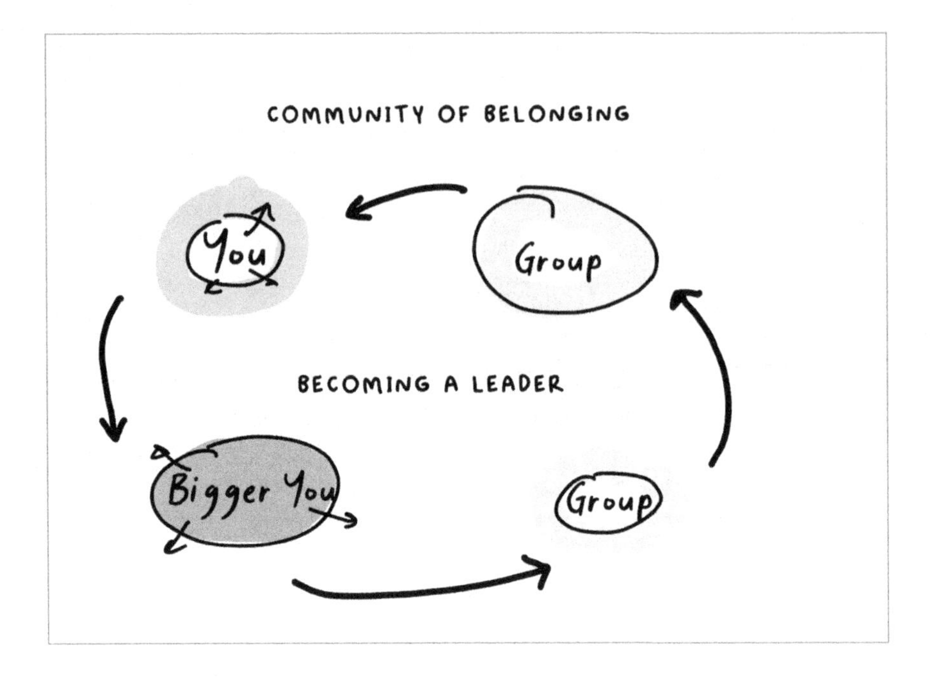

I described in the Wealth Dynamics section that wellness pros are usually some combination of star or creator personas, or supporter or mechanic. There are lots of other types, but these are by and far the most common I see.

The point is, you should lead your way. That will activate your wealth dynamic. Which may be different from my wealth dynamic.

Your group will drive you to lead. Leading will mean you are listening. The dynamic coaching conversation is your personalized leadership development program. You are being paid in the process of leading. Not bad.

6: Essential Sales Skills for Yoga Teachers

How to Enroll 1.6 People Per Month

Just to be crystal clear, you have a new problem.

Your new problem is how do you enroll 1.6 clients per month for $5000, month over month, for a yearly total of 20 members.

(Now if you're wanting to go from six figures to multiple six–change the numbers to meet your needs. For example 20 members at $12,000, or 50 members at $10,000. At first, the numbers will freak you out. That's normal. The numbers become normal the more you understand the value.)

(I included a sales video training with this book to guide you through this section.)

Now, the big leering question is refined to where are the 20 people who need you to guide them on this unique unicorn of a transformational journey going to come from?

No one's going to come to your house and make your dreams come true.

Grant Cardone, Sales Guru billionaire

My favorite exercise is to realize where your future members are already right now. Then, go there to meet them. That way you don't need to wait for your people to find you. In marketing, this is part of understanding your avatar–both the demographic and the psychographic.

Another of my favorite exercises is to find out where your avatar is currently spending that $5000, and not getting a very good return on that investment. That $5000 could be going down the drain. That $5000 could be spent on stuff that is aggravating their already below average health.

For instance, say you determine your avatar is a professional woman between 40-55 years old. Let's name her Jane. Jane earns over $80k per year. If she has a partner the household income is over $150k. She is 15-50 pounds overweight. She feels like she is trading time for money. Her periods and perimenopausal symptoms are getting more difficult to manage. She is having a hard time getting a good night's sleep. She has a gym membership. She likes hiking and yoga. Jane wishes she had a meditation practice to decrease her anxiety, but it never sticks. She eats out a few lunches and dinners out per week. Jane drinks at least a few bottles of wine per week. Her friendships are fun, but they aren't progressive. Jane enjoys a few vacations a year–to a tropical paradise or a ski trip. She always wishes she felt better in her bikini or ski pants.

Now, say in talking with Jane about what she most deeply wants in life she says the following: *I want to feel like I'm on top of my game. I want a raise. I know losing weight and getting better sleep would help me make that happen. I want more independence with my work. I want my salary and bonuses based on my performance. I want to feel in charge of my time and have more free time. I know I'm drinking too much wine, but it's hard to stop when my partner also enjoys wine. I really just want to feel in charge of my life and on top of my game. I don't want to keep going in the direction I'm currently heading–more wine, more weight and hitting my head on the glass ceiling. When I go on vacation I want to look great, but most of all I want to feel great in my body.*

Say you talk to Jane about the group you are forming. That you'll be guiding a Body Wisdom Club–a breakthrough group, to have the best years of their life now. The tuition is $420 a month for 12 months. Let's find the money in your current monthly expenses, so you can make a good investment in yourself. It'll pay back in spades for decades.

Sales Skills for Yoga Teachers

One of my favorite exercises is finding the money. You might say this is a reallocation exercise. You are looking for where the money is currently going. First look for costs that feed inflammation–like eating out, convenience foods and alcohol. Next, look for costs that are a result of the inflammation - like income plateauing, supplements and retail therapy. You can also look for high cost items that have a low return on her end goals, like expensive vacations. Say for Jane, you go through the costs and discover:

- Food Waste & Eating Out: $2400/year
- Tropical Trip: $5000/year
- Wine: $2500/year
- Supplements: $1200/year
- Income Plateau: $4000/year ($40k for 10 years)

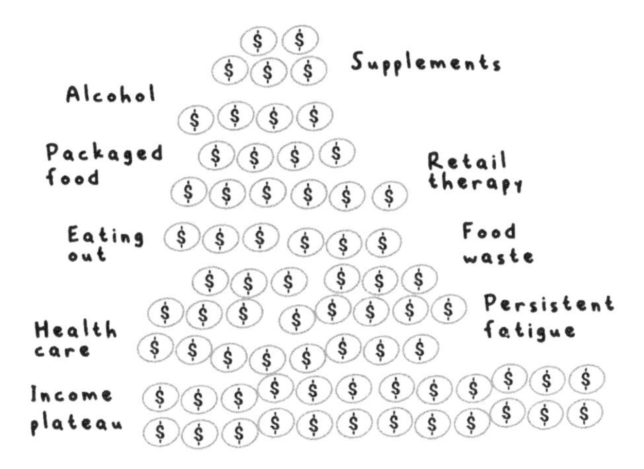

As you see above, the biggest cost for Jane is the opportunity cost of income plateau. This is common with chronic inflammation due to fatigue and the lack of focus and ambition that accompanies the systemic condition. Jane isn't confident in her body. She isn't getting good sleep. She doesn't seem to be performing as well at work. Because she is a career professional, she has an opportunity in the marketplace to increasingly earn higher performance pay. A 5% raise at her $80000 a year job is $4000.

If she were to wake up to her potential, dial in her body rhythms and live healthier habits, it's not at all unreasonable to believe she could increase her salary by $20,000 a year over the next few years. There are plenty of examples of how this happens every year, in every industry, in any economy. Being on top of your game and becoming increasingly useful in whatever is currently happening earns rewards in the professional marketplace. If Jane is under-slept and bloated with sugar from wine, you'll miss growth opportunities on a daily basis.

You may need to lead a journey before you witness the reality of this opportunity cost. As you empower people by empowering their habits, their opportunities take on a much better trajectory.

When you talk to Jane you'll want to ask her to describe what winning would look like to her. You'll need to give it the twelve month time frame, because we've already determined that that is enough time to get big results. You need to do this BEFORE you talk about your unique unicorn of a transformational journey.

You can use the Dan Sullivan question, "Jane, if we were having this conversation twelve months from today, and you were looking back at the past twelve months, what would have needed to happen for you to feel happy with your results?"

Then you listen.
You listen hard.

You make sure you learn and reflect back all aspects of what winning looks like for Jane in 12 months. Take notes so you can be sure of where she is starting now (A) and where she wants to be (B) in her own words. Understand what is stopping her from getting there on her own.

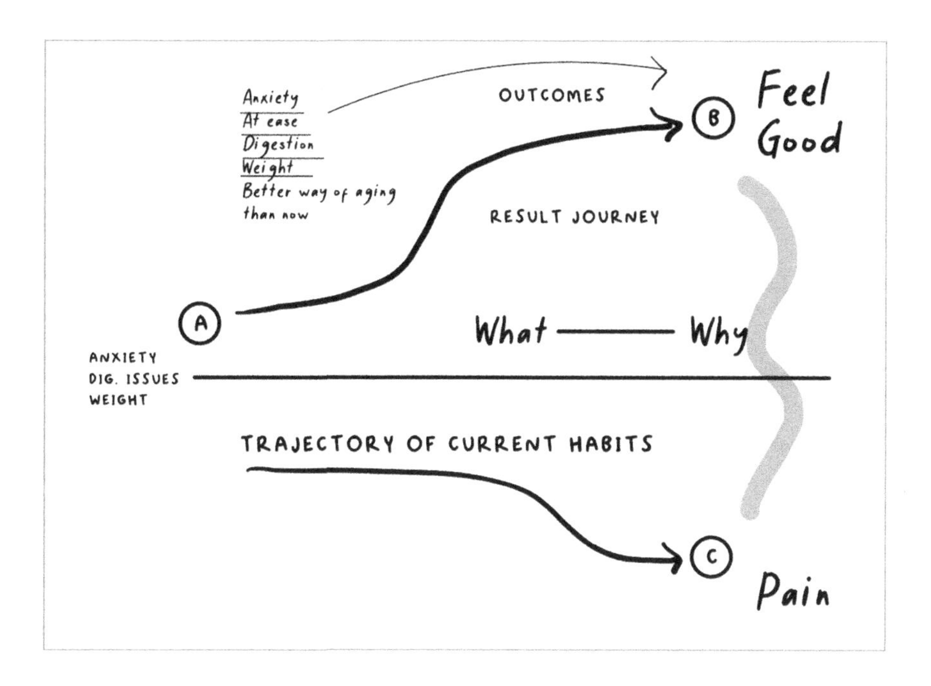

The big question for you is do you believe you could get Jane to excellent results in one year? Remember how you would guide her over the course of the year. Recall what is included in your package to get her to results.

If so, the big question for Jane, for her to make this huge leap in her life is, how tired is she of being stuck? Tired enough to invest in a new path for herself?

Make sure Jane is aware she is making a choice. Either life is on top of her, or she is on top of life.

A choice must be made. Her old way of investing her money isn't getting her what she wants. Is she uncomfortable enough to change her pattern of investing?

Then, check in with your gut, with your heart.

How, specifically, does your journey solve her problems? Ask her about, if she is part of a club of fun, progressive professionals who are all drinking less, cooking healthier and losing weight, if that would be helpful. Ask her if weekly check ins and action steps would help her. Ask her targeted questions that connect how you might help her with how she has already identified she needs to change.

If so, you can say something like, "Jane, based on what you've told me about how you're feeling, where you're stuck, and what you could reasonably do if you felt great, it sounds like we should get you on track to feeling great."

Ask her if she wants to hear how you could help her. Then, pause. She will say yes. Most people don't ask this question before presenting a solution. It's a crucial question. You should be invited to share your solution, rather than going into it uninvited.

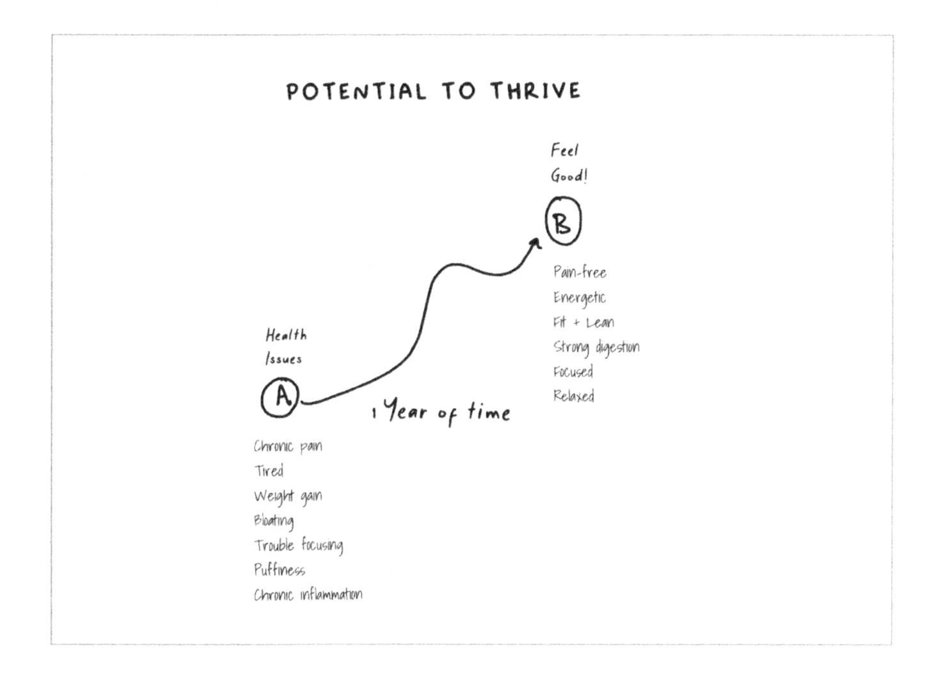

If yes, tell her you'll be guiding a Body Wisdom Club–a breakthrough group, to have the best years of their life now. Tell her specifically in ways that relate back to her current challenges. Ask her, if she trusts you as a leader and participated whole heartedly in your journey, what might happen for her? The tuition is $420 a month for 12 months. Directly ask her "Does my Body Wisdom Club sound like an effective plan of action to you?"

If Jane says "Yes", then ask her if she is ready for you to guide her into feeling great.

Now that you know who Jane is, the next question is where do you find 20 Jane's? Jane has friends and colleagues. Jane also has psychographics and demographics, perhaps, of the people you feel most called to serve. Some yoga teachers wig out about marketing (not to mention sales, but I'm beating that with a stick at this point). Marketing is simply being helpful for free.

Understand there is a process by which leads become members.

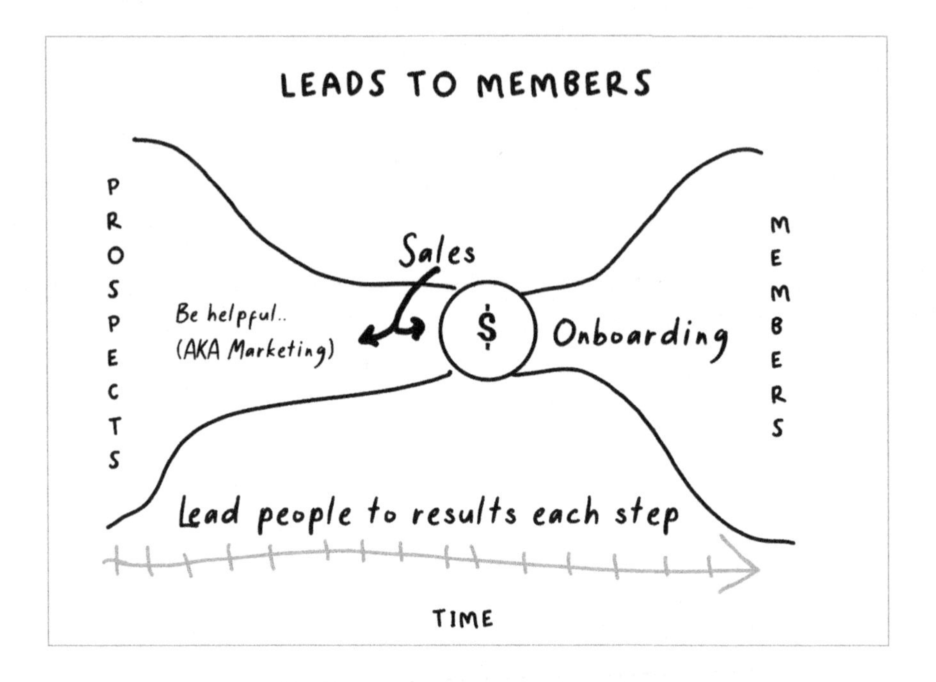

The process of engaging a lead is to find out what health issues they have, to be interested in assessing if you could help them feel good in a year, and to make sure they know you offer a journey that would get them to results. The entire procedure of attracting prospects, discovering their personal next level needs, and helping them invest in themselves is a step by step process that ultimately prepares the prospect in their new role as a course member.

In my courses, membership has responsibilities. We have a dynamic group culture to attune to. We have ground rules for dynamic groups. We prepare leads to step onto a moving bus, so that they can ride the momentum of the group to easier and faster results.

Respecting the function of each stage of the process is critical to your overall success. When each stage moves the lead towards experiencing what a group member experiences, there is a magnetic pull to being part of exactly what they have been looking for, though they didn't even know it existed, before they found you.

The video sales training that is included in this book will get you on your way.

Find Your Future Members

Remember earlier when I mentioned that your future members are looking for a breakthrough. Your power to find your 20 Janes is determined by how much responsibility you are willing to assume in finding her. Assume your responsibility is to find her and align your actions accordingly. She exists and needs you to find her.

Ask yourself, where does Jane spend time? Chances are, Jane is on Facebook and Instagram. As a professional, Jane is also on LinkedIn. Jane sees a doctor annually who makes holistic wellness referrals. Jane's company also offers lunch and learns, where people can give free talks. Jane's gym also offers spaces to teach workshops.

The question is *where* do you want to go to find Jane?

When I worked locally, I became known locally by doing free talks regionally at yoga studios, holistic health clinics, and even health food stores. When I shifted my work to online journeys I ran a simple advertising campaign on Facebook that targeted people like Jane.

You could make an online quiz: "Is your health in the way of your next raise?" and run ads to the quiz. You could do a free talk or make a tipsheet on "How to Get a Better Night Sleep to Feel Light + Look Great". You could do this locally, at the gym, at the women's health center, at the yoga studio. Or you could run a simple advertising campaign on Facebook, targeting Jane's demographics and psychographics, that follows up with an email campaign. However, I've found the best way is putting in sweat equity into word of mouth and referrals.

Once you have your prospects attention you want to more fully understand their challenges. To do that, you need to set up a 1-1 conversation. You want to know their specific challenges and goals.

This kind of conversation is the beginning of your sales training. It's not in the scope of this book to go thoroughly into sales training. We find in YHC it takes a few months of intensive training for most yoga teachers to get good at this skill, and about a year to become masterful.

Remember, sales are necessary skill if you are self-employed. Sales fall under the category of sales generating activities. Sales generating activities are what will sell out your seats. If you are committed to leading a transformative journey–know that the transformation gets traction in the sales conversation.

Meaning all sales conversations will make you a better journey leader. The day I looked at sales at my yoga studio, was the day I started to love the process of guiding people to invest in a better future for themselves.

Once you realize what is truly at stake for the person who has health challenges, that are leading to poor health, you may care enough to clear the hurdles that keep the person from investing in what will move them to feeling good in real time. Remember–you are helping them see they have two choices. B is the feel good in your future choice. C is the choice of making no choice. C is the choice to continue to have health issues that are compounded by their current habits over time.

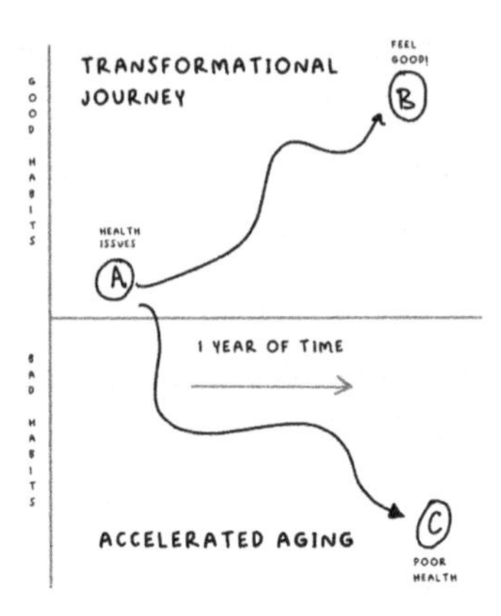

If you're afraid to talk about money, that is a hurdle you'll need to clear. You'll clear it in sales training, role playing and in practice. Perhaps you had the hurdle of your first backbend or headstand. Or perhaps the hurdle of teaching your first yoga classes. You're designed to clear hurdles through practice and continual improvement. When your yoga becomes your sales generating activities ... you'll move into financial freedom. This freedom is otherwise impossible for the self-employed wellness pro.

Now, assuming we're now on the same page with the sales mindset and sales generating activities, you'll need to talk to people one on one. While some people are hesitant to talk to people who can help them, others are not. For those who are hesitant to schedule a 1-1 complimentary session to find out their challenges and their goals, you'll want to discover how to overcome their hesitation. Usually I find that text messaging at some point leads naturally to a zoom meeting or phone conversation. At some point it makes sense to even a hesitant person to have a conversation. At that point you've earned their trust and they see the potential value in talking with you.

Then, you'll have the conversation like we outlined above with Jane. A very simple way to do this is to hold a series of talks–one per month–to generate roughly five leads per month. With five leads per month, you should easily enroll your almost two people per month. Bam. You will have the best work of your life helping your 20 Janes, and a lucrative lifestyle.

Here is how it works for Erica, a YHC member, "Literally every discussion or referral goes straight into a strategy session (in a loving, receiving, open-hearted way). I have three sales calls this week, that are as far as I can tell, largely "yes" ... all think my offer is super reasonable, one is taking time adjust some expenses, but expects to be on board at the end of the month! My point is that, I've never focused on sales being #1, but thanks to this training, even in the midst of chaos, my dreams of a lucrative practice is coming real! And my sales skills, which were previously non-existent seem to be improving!"

To make this book work for you, ascertain what you need to do to make this happen. Here are my final questions for you to answer:

- What are you going to need to know that you don't know? (Ex.sales generating activities)
- Where are you going to be challenged? (Ex. generating leads, giving free talks, sales conversations, closing)
- Where have you stopped before? (Ex. Raising my rates, building a package, sales)
- Where are you going to stop? (Be honest. If you won't invest in sales training or training like YHC in how to do this method, then acknowledge that.)

Where do you need to start?

The Janes of the world need people like you to embark on a truly transformational journey. She needs you to set a price point that is high enough for her to have skin in the game. High enough for her to pay attention to commit to her goals and your guidance.

> Your client needs you to set your price high enough for her to take the actions that will overcome her current habits, and lead her straight to her desired results.

In this book, I've covered why good habits matter for your yoga students, why you want to guide transformational journeys, how to design and price your journey, why your right avatar will pay a premium for the results to be guided by you and how to attract your avatar.

Maybe you've already tried to do this in the past and it hasn't worked out for you. Maybe you designed the experience for Jane, but didn't prioritize finding her. Maybe you found her, but didn't understand how to enroll her.

The most important thing for you to realize now is that this works for yoga teachers who invested in their money making skills. The economic value ladder is time-tested and reliable. You've got to get really clear on where your issues arise. You may need a coach or a guide to help you navigate those specific issues, because if someone can help you work through those issues, it's going to be worth it. If you don't transform, you don't get to earn more.

If you do, you'll always earn more.

In all the work I've done guiding yoga teachers to a more successful career, I've found that if you want to help people, there are plenty of people who need helping. Focus on being helpful. Commit to leading results to the transformational journey.

Use this method to up your game. Confront your demons along the way, and get on to the best work of your life.

7. Example of Packages, Pricing + Journeys

Packages

> Courage can be developed. But it cannot be nurtured in an environment that eliminates all risks, all difficulty, all dangers. It takes considerable courage to work in an environment in which one is compensated according to one's performance. Most affluent people have courage. What evidence supports this statement? Most affluent people in America are either business owners or employees who are paid on an incentive basis.
>
> Dr. Thomas Stanley

Dr. Stanley is laying down a hard truth right there. "It takes considerable courage to work in an environment in which one is compensated according to one's performance." The question is–are you willing to be compensated based on your performance as not just a transformational guide, but also as a solopreneur?

If you are willing–and all it takes is dedicated willingness and skin in the game–then pricing gets to be a lot of fun.

We never notice much difference in our enrollment process at Yogahealer for course memberships when we raise our prices based on performance. The enrollment process is a set of skills we teach in Yoga Health Coaching.

If you've read this far, you're investing your attention in your success. Let's look at a few pricing strategies based on differentiated professional skills. In Yoga Health Coaching we've guided yoga teachers, healers, and all sorts of wellness professionals including nurses, doctors, midwifes, Ayurvedic practitioners, Chinese Medicine practitioners, body workers (I like the term body mechanics), massage therapists, physical therapists, mental health therapists, energy workers, to get better at packaging, sales, and coaching members to success in a dynamic group.

In this part, I'll share a few ways of packaging journeys based on professions. There is tremendous variability in pricing depending on results, which depends on expertise and experience.

YOGA TEACHER. Pilates Teacher. FITNESS INSTRUCTOR.TRAINER. Movement Professional.

A story...

When Monica first launched her pilot group she wanted to transition out of her day job at an institution and just focus on guiding people to feel much better. She priced at $4000, signed up 15 people, and had the revenue to quit her other job. What she couldn't believe was how much more time she had with her business than with her day job–for the same amount of income. She also knew she had leverage to expand her group, or expand the journey.

Her large living area would fit 15 people, and she wanted a familial atmosphere. She included club night in parties where she guided her members through interactive life-growth workshops using tools like liberating structures and collaborative learning. She worked out a deal with the yoga studio where she taught so that her 15 members could get her classes unlimited. She wanted a close relationship with her 15 members throughout the year. She also wanted her members to have access to her 1-1 work as a yoga therapist once a month for thirty minutes, and 30 minutes of personalized health coaching.

Monica's Club: 15 people at $4000

- Body habits coaching: Group weekly
- Four, two day intensive retreats
- 12 club night parties
- Unlimited yoga classes with Monica
- 1-1 habit coaching and yoga therapy: monthly check-ins
- Group forum
- Video library - General and personalized

BOUTIQUE STUDIO OR GYM OWNER (YOGA/PILATES/CROSSFIT MOVEMENT)

A story...

Leanne had a small yoga studio that fit twenty mats in a medium size town in Texas. She had just turned 70 when we met in Yoga Health Coaching. Leanne's following as a teacher was mostly women from age 50-75, who loved her infectious inspiration and body knowledge in the classroom.

Leanne knew she could fit 20 people, and that was it. Plus, she didn't want to work a lot. Her group filled fast. Having the container of the journey, having the one upsell, the one offer, meant she didn't have to put on so many workshops or other events to help her most commitment members. Because she loved doing local retreat-like intensive at her studio, she included four weekends of retreats for her members. She wanted her members to recruit new members, so she included eight, bring a friend member mixer free talks, based on topics that her members wanted to learn more about.

Leanne's Club: 20 people at $6500

- Body habits coaching: Group weekly
- Four, two day intensive retreats
- 8 bring a friend member mixer free talks
- Unlimited yoga classes
- 1-1 coaching: monthly check-ins
- Group forum
- Video library - General and personalized

BIG STUDIO OR GYM OWNER (YOGA/PILATES/CROSSFIT/MOVEMENT)

A story...

Mari and Tom had a yoga studio and gym with three rooms and three bodywork treatment rooms. They could fit 50 mats in their largest room. Their gym had a staff of 10 teachers, who all operated as contractors. They were the only employees in the business, and both Mari and Tom had backgrounds in exercise physiology, personal training and yoga.

They knew their members needed a habits and lifestyle coaching component. They also realized they had no upsell to their fitness classes, and were therefore hustling to make every dollar. For their general pass, they wanted a big group–50 people!

The already had one day intensives going at their gym, that were unpredictable to fill. They decided to leverage their overhead and all the activities they were trying to fill. They wanted their members to have access to all classes and to be able to reserve a spot in workshops.

They know their people are busy, and can't attend everything anyway, so why not have lots of options. Their gym also had a big kitchen Mari wanted to use for healthy eating classes.

GYM JOURNEY Club: 50 people at $5000

- Body habits coaching: Group weekly
- Unlimited fitness classes
- Six, one day intensive retreats
- Bring a friend mixer free workshops
- Access to specific workshops or cooking classes
- Unlimited fitness classes
- Group forum
- Video library - general and personalized

Mari and Tom knew they could leverage their relationships with teachers, trainers and therapists with a VIP pass that included one on one work.

GYM VIP Club: 10 people at $10,000

- Body habits coaching: Group weekly
- Unlimited fitness classes
- Personal training package
- Bodywork/Yoga therapy package
- Six one- day intensive retreats
- Bring a friend mixer free workshops
- Access to specific workshops
- Group forum
- VIP health coaching 1-1 sessions
- Video library - General and personalized

Physical Therapist. BODY MECHANIC. Yoga Therapist. Midwife. Detox therapist. Private Retreats.

A story...

Ann wanted to transition from her life's work in midwifery. She knew deep down there was a next level of her career. She knew a lot about herbalism, yoga, and women's body wisdom. She decided to lead a women's empowerment group. Her first year in Yoga Health Coaching - which guided her to transition her career–she earned more money and had more fun, without the late nights of midwifery work. The second year, she increased her price, based on results, and continues to break her personal records for rewarding work and income. She loved leading ritual events - and made that the cornerstone of getting her group together in person.

Ann's JOURNEY Club: 25 people at $6500

- Body habits coaching: Group weekly
- Six, one day women's wisdom + ritual workshops intensives
- 3 day body empowerment retreat
- Group forum
- 1-1 health coaching sessions
- Video library - General and personalized

A story...

Jack was an all star body mechanic. When we met, Jack had 30 years, yes, 30 as a massage therapist. He also was an Ayurvedic practitioner and detox specialist for 10 years, and had just completed training as an osteopath. Jack was plenty busy when we met, his schedule packed with clients. However, Jack was frustrated because there was no leverage in his business. He was trading time for money. Also, his private retreat detox clients would have a tremendous experience, but were not able to maintain their results on their own.

Jack packaged the journey to guide to results. He knew his patients needed life skills, breathing skills, cooking skills, and movement skills. He brought these skills in with a video library, and with two three-day live events at a local gym that also had a kitchen. He realized he only wanted to work at this depth with 15 people per year.

JACK'S JOURNEY: 15 people at $15k

- 6 day private intensive Ayurvedic detox (Pancha Karma)
- Body habits coaching: Group Weekly
- Group forum
- Two, three day super skill building workshop
- 1-1 health coaching sessions
- Video library - General and personalized

Mark's Peak Performance Package

A story...

Mark was a world class physical therapist. He was tired of working on rich people and wanted to return working with athletes. As we talked, it became obvious to me that what Mark really wanted was to work with peak performers. Peak performers show up in all arenas of life - from corporate board rooms to professional sports to amateur competitors.

Mark built his package for someone those who had plenty of incentive to invest in their body, and who wanted a world class body mechanic. He realized he was missing the health coaching component. He also realized he hadn't packaged his services to get either commitment, investment or to incentivize his patients to get long term results.

When Mark realized he wanted to work with peak performers, he knew these people valued their time above all else. A journey must be tailored to the needs of the members. His members wanted reminders, motivation, and personalized health concierge services to coordinate finding trainers on the road and working with other service providers

PEAK PERFORMERS PASS: 10 people at $25k

- 25 bodywork sessions (1-1)
- Bi-weekly text check ins
- 25 body habits coaching sessions (1-1)
- Weekly office hours
- Video library - General and personalized
- Group forum
- Concierge services with other health care professionals

MENTAL HEALTH THERAPIST. Psychologist.

A story...

J.C. had survived severe childhood trauma. Her grandfather helped her get to college and she excelled in writing. On her healing path she found dance, fitness, yoga. On her pro journey she became a mental health therapist. In YHC she put together an annual pass–she led the journey. And she started her book to help others with PTSD.

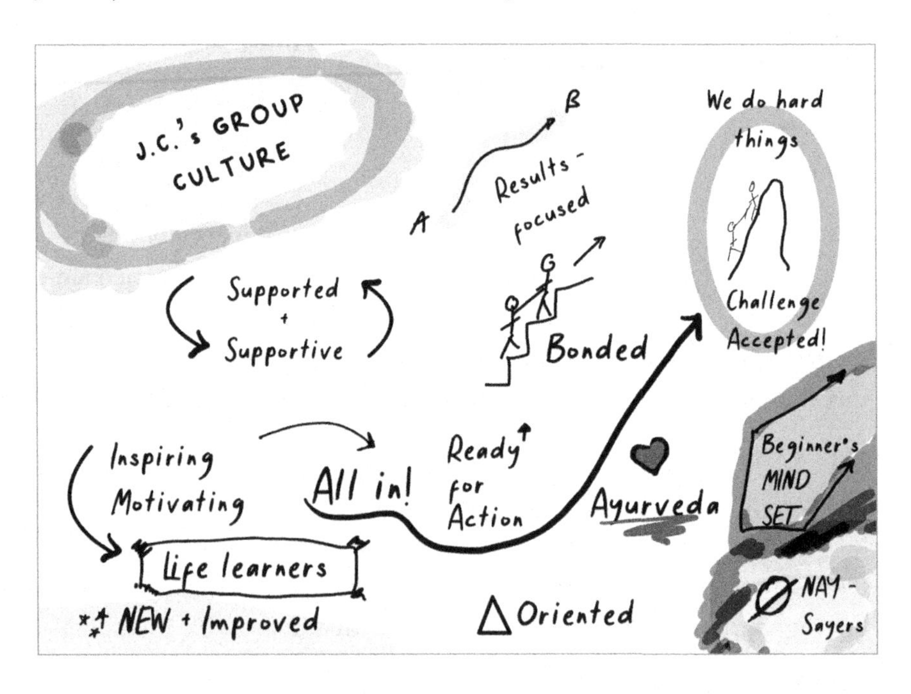

From Yoga Health Coaching, she learned how to run dynamic group interaction sessions. She found that her therapy clients loved the interaction. She noticed that the members were able to focus forward, make small changes that had big results, and that she her therapy skills and love of movement and physical health were finally all combined into one offering.

J.C.'s Club: 20 people at 5,000

- Body habits coaching: Group Weekly
- Monthly movement + magic workshops intensives
- Group forum
- 1-1 health coaching sessions
- Video library with movement and dance videos

NURSE

A story...

Annette was a lifelong nurse at a hospital. She had raised her three kids. She loved yoga and had a yoga teaching side hustle. Her students adored her. She looked great. She felt tired. Tired of nursing. Tired of the hospital. Tired of doling out prescriptions. Her personal habits were so different. When we met it was clear that Annette was frustrated she couldn't make an impact with her wellness wisdom at work. More and more she saw that degenerative habits are what brought patients into hospitals, and she wanted to keep people out of the hospital!

When Annette first joined YHC she kept her day job. She got her group off the ground, online, even while moving across country for her husband's work and their dream of living in California. She loved the transformational journey business model. She got her coaching business off the ground, quit her day job and never looked back. She fell in love with Ayurveda, aromatherapy and skin care, and added personalized products to her journey package.

- Body habits coaching: Group weekly
- 3 day intensive training sessions (Online or in person)
- 1-1 coaching: monthly check-ins
- Video library - general and personalized
- Personalized skin care
- Personalized aromatherapy

Nutritionist. Ayurvedic Practitioner. Chinese Medicine Practitioner.

A story...

Lorena had troubling acne as a teen and young adult. This started her on a healing journey in Ayurveda. When we met she had already completed her training. She was determined to help young women invest in their body wisdom and lead them the life skills she wished she had, without needing to become practitioners.

- Body habits coaching: Group Weekly
- 3 day intensive training sessions (Online or in person)
- Skin care workshops
- Yoga workshops
- Personalized herbal formulas
- Personalized therapeutic sessions
- 1-1 Health Coaching: monthly check-ins
- 2 Group Guided Detoxes a Year
- Video Library - General and personalized
- Personalized herbal formulas

Lead *YOUR* Journey

You get to guide the journey only you can guide. With the free toolkit that goes with this book - we'll help you. You can receive a 1-1 coaching session with us to review what you should offer in your journey, based on your expertise.

8. Beliefs That Breed Success

Four Beliefs that Follow the Spiritual Laws of Financial Success

> Sometimes you put walls up not to keep people out, but to see who cares enough to break them down.
>
> Socrates

To guide transformation you need to build a wall that separates your members into your own club. Inside your journey you can contain and support your members. Build a journey, a container, a structure, a wall, to separate the inside from the outside, the committed from the complacent. Containers are crucial for providing the structure that enable personal and collective evolutions.

Socrates made a stand for developing one's wisdom and stating one's beliefs, like his belief around why to put up walls. In conclusion, I'll review beliefs that I've arrived at through twenty years of experience at Yogahealer.com. Before I review the core beliefs that will help you with your mindset, I want to ask yourself the following questions:

- What are your core beliefs about your career as a yoga teacher?
- What are your core beliefs around your work?
- What are your core beliefs about your next purpose?

These core beliefs will serve you in being more effective and more successful as a yoga teacher.

Core Belief #1: Daily habits are the deal breaker between the global epidemic of chronic systemic inflammation vs. feeling good while aging.

As a yoga teacher, you can make a stand for better habits for your students to shift from modern health issues to feeling good. Yoga Teachers who lead their members into smarter habits get better results faster.

As a yoga teacher, you are perfectly positioned to guide members to feeling much better, much faster, when you lead a journey based on the good habits, which are the backbone of the yoga practice.

> Health is the effect of a healthy lifestyle and healthy habits. Disease is the tree sprouted from unhealthy habits.
>
> Dr. Vasant Lad, Ayurvedic guru

Core Belief #2: Yoga teachers who want to break their glass ceilings need to invest in career training.

The most essential career training is in packaging the journey, sales skills, attraction skills, and dynamic groups ... in that order.

There's a reason most yoga teachers reinforce their own glass ceilings and get stuck. Usually, yoga teachers aren't attracted to investing in career training. They invest in more yoga training–thinking if they are a better teacher they'll earn more. Or they invest in another modality–like a specific therapeutic training, like massage, Ayurveda, aromatherapy, herbalism. If they do invest in business training, it's usually general business training, ant not a specific coaching, sales and marketing model for someone who knows the wellness-pro lifestyle business model like explained here.

The internet is a very competitive place. Needing fewer students, clients or members is essential for most yoga teachers who want a wellness lifestyle ... not a business lifestyle. Career success is a different kind of wisdom, usually both undervalued and under-invested.

Core Belief #3: People transform faster in better company.

This is true both for you as a yoga teacher who can join Yoga Health Coaching, and for your prospects who can get a ticket for your journey. As business guru Jim Rohn says, "Don't join an easy crowd. You won't grow. Go where the expectation and demands to perform are high."

Being with better company–the company of people for who are guiding a transformational journey–who are mastering sales and attraction, who are astounded at their group's progress, would accelerate your progress.

Just like you wouldn't expect your clients to get healthier on their own, don't expect yourself to navigate next level career success flying solo. Too many yoga teachers try to figure it out on their own. Collaborative learning is proven to result in higher achievement, better retention, better ideas, faster learning, and higher level reasoning than traditional learning.

Look at your past as a wellness journey. Investigate your past as a yoga teacher. You'll see that you probably didn't join an easy crowd. Especially those of you who are very good at what you do. You probably invested in the best yoga training (and the best conversation) that you could find. You found a way to make it work financially. I bet you joined your yoga training wholeheartedly. I would also bet that there was an expectation that you would grow, that you would perform, that you would show up, that you would behave in certain ways. And I would bet that you stepped up to fulfill that expectation.

Now this same is true for your financial success. We actually need to join a crowd where exceptional financial success is normal. Perhaps join a crowd of people grow their potential, their income and design their lifestyle, year over year. In my circle, this behavior is expected.

Because if we're not in that crowd, it's not normal to earn more. It's not normal to learn more about a better business model or to grow into it. If you're in the crowd where it's normal to not grow, where it's normal to earn the same year over year, despite having more experience, then your behaviors and personality will cement around that limited reality. You may start to think that you don't have what it takes. You may think the current market only values yoga teachers so much. That breaks my heart. The sky is the limit. Aim high.

Value your wisdom at a premium. Prove your value by leading a journey to results.

Discipline to the Target

> It's better to hang out with people better than you. Pick out associates whose behavior is better than yours and you'll drift in that direction."[1]
>
> Warren Buffett

To Warren Buffett's point–you've been hanging out with me reading this book. I hope by now the possibility of you leading a transformational journey and earning based on results is top of mind for you. Leave this book with a specific goal, and a discipline to that goal.

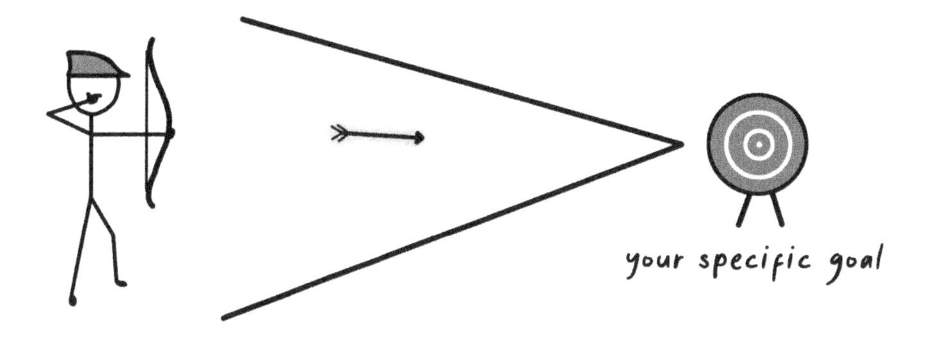

To identify your goal, and further drift in this direction, I have four essential questions for you. There are no right or wrong answers. There are simply your inner truths. Wrap up this process by summarizing what you discovered in this book:

1. How badly do you want to lead people to feeling good?
2. What would you do with a more established authority in helping people feel good?
3. How much money do you want to make next year?
4. What would you do with more money?

If you don't take time to answer the four questions above, pitfalls will arise. The first pitfall is you won't know what is at stake. If you aren't honest with yourself about what is at stake, you won't change. Is that worth $15k? $50k? $100k? $250k? Only you can invest in you.

> Your greatness is limited only by the investments you make in yourself.
>
> Grant Cardone, Sales Entrepreneur Billionaire

The second pitfall is that you won't clarify or articulate your ambition to help people with what you know. To me, your ambition is sacred. To me, what you most deeply want is as close to a divine directive as it gets.

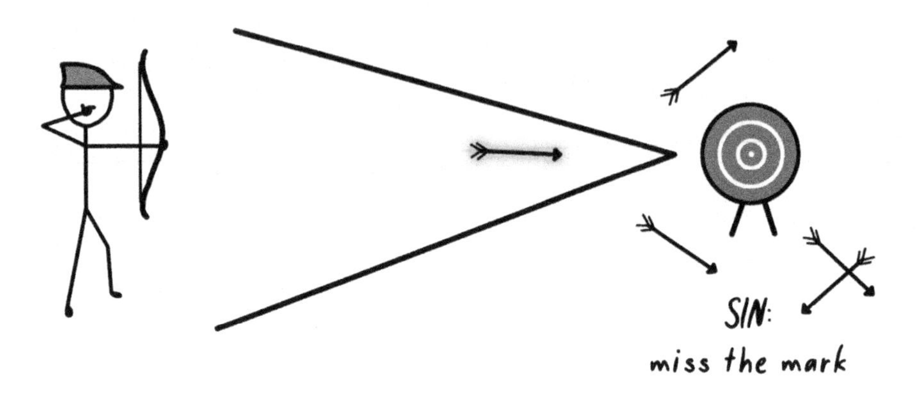

> If you won't clarify your true ambitions you can't achieve the level of meaning in your life. Your ambition is sacred. Honor your ambition. Protect it. Serve it.

I watched many seasoned yoga teachers give up on their true ambitions. Ambitions of impact. Ambitions of financial savings. Ambitions of a certain lifestyle. Ambitions around depth of study. Ambitions of leadership. As Qui-Gon Jinn said in Star Wars: "Your focus determines your reality."

I want to leave you with the magic that is possible within your membership group. I'll share an image below from mapping out YHC member JC's group culture. JC was clear that the group culture she would create for her members would have balance, her intensity to be all in, do hard things and be ready for action, with being supported, loving Ayurveda and bonding.

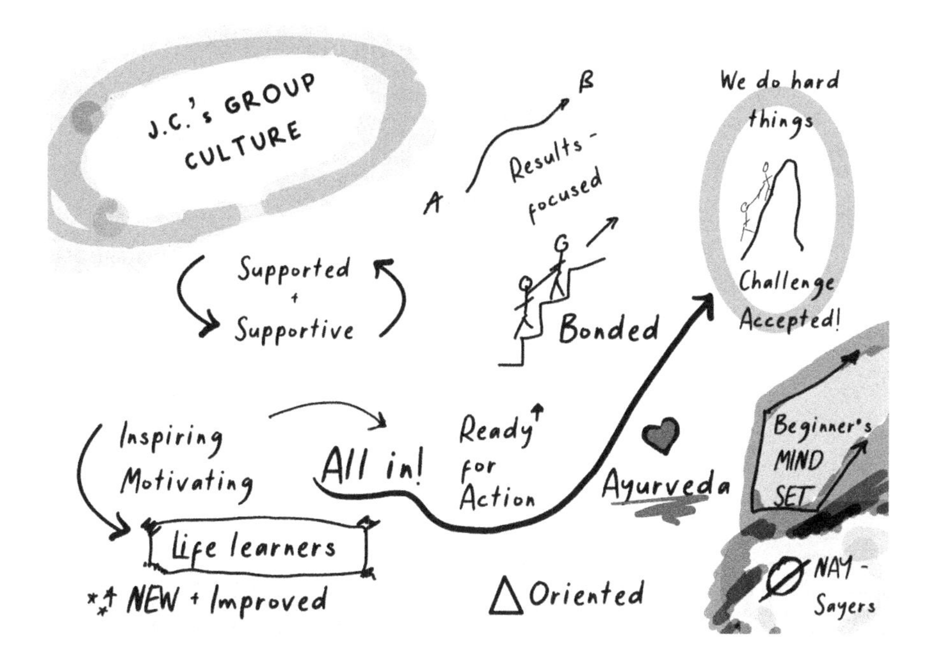

This is the process of making your members journey real. You create what you think would be the best experience ever. Then, you get to test it. with your pilot You'll improve it in motion as you enroll your next quarter. This is the earn while you learn.

As I guided JC to tap into the group culture that she most wanted to be part of, to create and to lead ... her ambition sparked. She could see her purpose. Her purpose was to provide a unique club a life-changing experience. She saw how this would evolve her personality as a leader. She could see how her personal habits, in how she would run her career, would need to radically evolve. And she was up for the challenge.

JC also realized that this is how it would be for her members. She would guide her members to be clear on their purpose. She could focus her mom members on the person and personality they would be evolving into. The purpose could be achieved with the specific habits that would develop that improved aspect of their personality. She knew this was a call to do the most important work of her life.

You'll be happiest and most useful when you do your best work, when you guide the most profound transformation, when your members have skin in the game for you to earn and lead well. When you can guide people to get what they want faster, you dramatically alter the trajectory of their lives ... and yours.

Endnotes

Health Issues Facing Modern Humans

1. **Chronic Inflammation**
   Roma Pahwa; Amandeep Goyal; Pankaj Bansal; Ishwarlal Jialal.
   2020 https://www.ncbi.nlm.nih.gov/books/NBK493173/#

Symptoms of Chronic Inflammation

1. **Chronic Inflammation**
   Roma Pahwa; Amandeep Goyal; Pankaj Bansal; Ishwarlal Jialal.
   2020 https://www.ncbi.nlm.nih.gov/books/NBK493173/#

What are the 6 Habits Yoga Teachers Shouldn't Have?

1. Lad, V. (2002). Textbook of Ayurveda: Volume one. Albuquerque, N.M: Ayurvedic Press.

What is in Your High Ticket Item?

1. (Note, in Yoga Health Coaching we provide YHC's with a member hub for their new members with the trainings used by our entire community. We've found, over time, that the pressure of creating their unique materials before their group gets going. We've found that it's better to focus on enrolling your pilot group, and getting off the ground, then focusing on building training videos.)

Price your Ticket

1. Willpower Doesn't Work by Benjamin Hardy

Discipline to the Target

1. https://www.thegentlemansjournal.com/what-warren-buffett-wants-you-to-invest-in/#:

Resources

As a bonus with this book purchase, you can get access to Cate's **6-Figure Yoga Teacher TOOLKIT** . Cate walks you through the concepts in this book. This toolkit is worth a bundle. You get it free! It includes a career assessment and a one on one consultation and video training from Cate's studio. http://www.yogahealthcoaching.com/toolkit

This free Toolkit guides you to:

- Take action to have your best year ever, financially
- Adopt the most effective business model used by financially successful yoga teachers
- Find your unique voice
- Discover what your students most need from you

Listen to Cate on her *Yogahealer Podcast, Yoga Health Coaching Podcast*

Also by CATE STILLMAN

Body Thrive Uplevel Your Body and Your Life with the 10 Habits from Ayurveda and Yoga

Master of You A Five-Point System to Synchronize Your Body, Your Home and Your Time with Your Ambition

About the Author

CATE STILLMAN has guided a global online community at Yogahealer.com to thrive in body and in life through innovative yoga and Ayurvedic teachings since 2001.

She hosts the Yogahealer Podcast and Yoga Health Coaching podcast, weekly podcasts on thought leadership, with simple solutions for humans to be healthier. Cate is the author of Body Thrive and Master of You with Sounds True Publishing. An avid mountain biker, skier and surfer, her family splits their time between Wyoming and Mexico. For free workshops, check out yogahealer.com and listen to her podcast.

ABOUT YOGA HEALTH COACHING (YHC)

YHC is a training program that guides yoga teachers and wellness professionals into a better business model, better client results and a great work/life balance lifestyle. YHC is a certification course focused on implementing the Lead the Journey business model in real time, while earning a return on investment during the first year. Some members quadruple their tuition investment in the first quarter year.

All members love the transition from teaching into leading the transformational journey.

To start our Lead the Journey course, email info@yogahealthcoaching.com, subject line: I want to lead a journey.

Made in the USA
Coppell, TX
31 January 2022